Douglas A-1
Skyraider

OSPREY AIR COMBAT

Douglas A-1
Skyraider

Robert F Dorr

Published in 1989 by Osprey Publishing Limited
59 Grosvenor Street, London W1X 9DA

British Library Cataloguing in Publication Data

Dorr, Robert F 1939—
    Douglas A-1 Skyraider.
    1. Aeroplanes. Skyraider, A-1 McDonnell
Douglas
    I. Title
    623.74'64

ISBN 0-85045-906-0

Editor Dennis Baldry
Design by Gwyn Lewis
Filmset in Great Britain by Tameside Filmsetting
Limited, Ashton-under-Lyne, Lancashire and printed
by BAS Printers Limited, Over Wallop, Hampshire

FRONT COVER
*AD-6 Skyraider of VA-115 skims the waves during a
sortie from USS Shangri-La (CVA-38) in 1959. '510' is
also featured in the colour section on page 64*

BACK COVER
*The impressive hornet emblem used by the 'Thunderbolts' of
US Navy attack squadron VA-176, which was equipped
with Skyraiders during the Vietnam War (See page 148)*

Contents

Chapter 1
AD-1
The Dauntless II
and a Cat's Grace

In the mid-1940s it was pretty well understood that carrier-based warplanes were large blue machines with propellers hanging out in front. Engineers in other disciplines might be experimenting with a new fangled idea called jet propulsion, but no one really knew if an aeroplane that emitted hot air out of a tailpipe would be practical aboard an aircraft carrier. Someone had said that if God wanted jet airplanes to fly, he would have put propellers in front of them.

When the Navy looked around for a replacement for its SBD Dauntless, serious consideration was never given to any powerplant except the time-proven reciprocating engine.

The Dauntless, of course, requires no introduction. If it hadn't been for the SBD and its intrepid crews, all of us east of the International Dateline would be conversing today in, and this book would be written in, Japanese. The Battle of Midway was not merely a turning point of the war but a pivotal moment in the twentieth century. The battle was decided late in the afternoon, with daylight and fuel running out, the American naval aviators stretched to maximum distance from their carriers, plagued by mechanical problems, about to give up . . . when a hole opened in the clouds enabling Dauntlesses to swarm down on the Japanese carriers *Hiryu*, *Soryu*, *Kaga* and *Akagi*. In a brief shining moment, arguably the decisive moment of this century, a few brave men in a few Douglas Dauntlesses crippled the Emperor's carrier force and reversed the course of the Pacific conflict. The firebombing of Tokyo, the razing of Hiroshima and Nagasaki, were just icing on the cake.

A total of 5936 Dauntless dive-bombers were built. The Dauntless in its SBD-6 variant was powered by a 1350-hp (1007-kW) Wright R-1820-66 Cyclone 9 piston engine, was capable of 255 mph (410 km/h) at 14,000 ft (4265 m) and had underfuselage mountings for up to 1600 lb (726 kg) of bombs, a further 650 lb (295 kg) fitting under the wings.

Although Douglas' Ed Heinemann is often credited with the Dauntless design, the airplane truthfully was the result of Jack Northrop's influence on Douglas design philosophy. The Dauntless was a record-setter in terms of achievement and longevity, remaining the principal carrier-based scout/dive bomber throughout World War 2. It was also a reflection of a Navy mission. The dive-bombing role could have been performed by a single-seater but the scout mission, visual reconnaissance for the Fleet, required the second man in the rear seat, who also operated the Dauntless' radio and .30-calibre (7.62-mm) machine gun.

The hybrid scout/dive-bomber mission was not always performed as successfully as by the Dauntless. The nominal replacement for the Dauntless was the Curtiss SB2C Helldiver, stuck forever with the nickname The Beast and regarded as pretty beastly by a generation of naval aviators. It had 'more than its share of maligners', as one insider recalls and the best thing that can be said with certainty about the SB2C Helldiver is that it out-performed its own principal competitor, the Brewster SB2A Buccanneer. Out-performing the luckless Brewster was not a difficult feat and it remains difficult to find other praise for the Helldiver, but a few mavericks in the Fleet were at home in the portly animal—proving that if enough pilots fly an aircraft, some of them will love it.

Like the Dauntless, the Helldiver was a tail-dragger with a big round 'recip' engine, in this case the 1900-hp (1417 kW) Wright R-2600-20 Cyclone 14. No fewer than seven thousand Beasts rolled off the production lines and served with the Fleet, not bad for a machine which warrants mixed reviews at best. The SB3C aircraft, conceived in 1941 as insurance against failure of the Helldiver, ended up being built in mockup form only and thus was denied the opportunity to become the first US shipboard warplane with tricycle landing gear.

Dauntless Replacement

Even before Pearl Harbor, teething troubles with the SB2C Helldiver caused the Navy to briefly consider the unbuilt SB3C and to order the then-ageing Dauntless back into larger-scale production, so that the Dauntless and its replacement were pouring from factory lines almost simultaneously. An even mangier dog of an airplane, the Brewster SB2A, was kept in production as a backup.

Douglas made an early start on its own 'Dauntless replacement', the SB2D-1. At this time, the scout/dive-bomber mission was unchanged and a second crewman was needed in the rear of the aircraft to employ his Mark One Eyeball searching for the bad guys.

As early as June 1941, the Navy ordered two prototype SB2D-1 Destroyer aircraft. The first (bureau number 03551) flew on 8 April 1943. The Destroyer differed from all previous designs in having retractable tricycle landing gear, a feature which never proved successful with aircraft of this category.

The SB2D-1 has been described as 'clean and purposeful-looking', but even as it underwent testing, the Navy made a dramatic change in its definition of the intended mission. The 'scout' role was dropped from the Fleet's needs, dooming both the SB category of aircraft and the second crew member in the back seat.

ABOVE
Exhausted, low on fuel, running out of daylight, extended to maximum range from their carriers, a handful of SBD Dauntless dive-bomber pilots turned the tide at Midway and altered the course of the century. SBD-1 Dauntless (bureau number 1597) in early Marine Corps markings demonstrates the shape which became familiar on carrier decks in the Pacific (USN)

ABOVE RIGHT
The Curtiss SB2C Helldiver, chosen to replace the Dauntless, was 'a fine airplane in many respects', acknowledged Douglas's Ed Heinemann but was also 'heavier and more expensive than the Dauntless'. Intended to weigh 1200 lb (544 kg) less than the SBD, the SB2C ended up exceeding the Dauntless's weight by that figure. Those who loved the airplane and those who didn't called it The Beast (USN via R J Mills Jr)

A BT category, for a dive-bomber capable of carrying torpedoes, was introduced. The BT series of aircraft were to be single-seaters. Curtiss entered the competition with the BTC, of which more in a moment. Douglas entered the new mission sweepstakes by modifying the SB-2D-1, converting it to a single-seater and adding two wing-mounted 20-mm cannon, an enlarged internal bomb bay and increased fuel capacity. Powered by a 2300-hp (1715-kW)

Wright R-3350-14 Cyclone 18 engine, the power-plant which will be essential to the narrative which follows, the new aircraft emerged as the BTD. The first BTD-I resulted from a 31 August 1943 contract and was a nice-looking aircraft but, as an engineer recalls, 'it performed like a gigantic heap of dog turds'.

The BTD-I retained the name Destroyer. At one juncture, in a blush of optimism, the Navy ordered 358. Production BTD-I Destroyers began to reach the Navy in June 1944 but it is not thought that any ever joined an operational squadron or flew from a carrier. Only 28 (of 48 in the final version of the order) had been delivered when the contract was cancelled shortly after VJ Day.

In one of many attempts to get a better-performing BT-class airframe, two of these machines were provided experimentally with a mixed powerplant, a downward-angled 1580-lb (680-kg) thrust Westing-house WE-19XA turbojet being fitted in the rear fuselage and fed with air through a dorsal inlet aft of the cockpit. First flown in May 1945, the resulting BTD-2 Destroyer was the first jet-powered aircraft in the Navy. The jet installation was not successful under realistic conditions and the BTD-2 was never really in the running as the long-sought Dauntless replacement.

While the BTD was scrutinized by Navy planners, work proceeded on three other possible Dauntless

replacements, the Curtiss BTC, the Martin BTM, and the Kaiser Fleetwings BTK. In today's cost-conscious world, it would be inconceivable to have so many experimental prototype airplanes being test flown, but in the mid-1940s it was not unusual.

Curtiss-Wright's Columbus division had gotten a considerable head start on other manufacturers with a June 1942 proposal covering an R-3350-powered candidate as well as an alternate version using the more promising R-4360 Wasp Major.

Four experimental prototypes—two R-3350-powered BTC-1 and two R-4360-powered BTC-2 aircraft—were ordered by letter of intent in June 1942. Various difficulties, including production and early service problems with the previous generation's SB2C-1 Helldiver, led to a decision to cancel the BTC-1 and only the BTC-2 variant was proceeded with. Despite early progress, actual flight testing of the Curtiss machine was seriously delayed and the first BTC-2 did not get aloft until January 1945. By then, other events in the quest for a Dauntless replacement had left the BTC design behind, and the once-unbeatable Curtiss firm was well on its way towards being a *former* manufacturer of aircraft.

Despite difficulties with the designs from other companies, for a time it looked as if the manufacturer of the Navy's next airplane was going to be just anybody but Douglas. In June 1944, the Navy cancelled the BTD programme, concluding that the

ABOVE
The SB2D-1 Destroyer retained the 'scout' mission with a Dauntless-style rear seat crewman who, unfortunately, lacked the visibility to do very much scouting and needed remote control to operate his rearward-facing guns. Mercifully, the Navy dropped the 'scout' mission and the quest for a Dauntless replacement proceeded without the two-seat configuration (Douglas via Hal Andrews)

RIGHT
Perhaps the least likely candidate for a Dauntless replacement was the Brewster SB2A-1 Buccaneer, which was ordered into production in 1941 solely for insurance. The SB2A-1 never did serve in combat and the company which made it did not survive the war (USN via R J Mills Jr)

BTD-I was merely a warmed-over version of the SB2D and that Douglas's efforts were too long delayed and too rife with difficulties. It might have seemed to an observer that Martin would walk away with the big production orders.

Martin's Entry

The development of a new class of warplane must inevitably be a difficult undertaking, with more than a few false starts and unavoidable detours. As we continue this account of how the Dauntless led to the Skyraider, some attention must be given to the promising aircraft developed by the Glenn L Martin Company of Baltimore, Maryland, partly because that firm's candidate actually *did* reach squadron service (briefly) and influenced thinking for years thereafter.

The Martin Model 210 design proposal resulted in a contract for two BTM-I prototypes (bureau nos 85161/85162), the first of which flew on 26 August 1944. A cantilever low-wing monoplane with retractable 'tail dragger' gear, the BTM-I was powered by a 3000-hp (2237-kW) Pratt & Whitney R-4360 Wasp Major radial engine. Based on early tests and the exigencies of war, the Navy ordered 750 aircraft.

In due course, the Navy dropped the BT prefix. The Martin aircraft was redesignated AM and given the nickname Mauler. The first production AM-I Mauler (bureau no 22257)—to get ahead of our story—made its initial flight on 16 December 1946.

The heaviest and largest airplane ever built for operation from a carrier deck, the Mauler had a gross weight of 19,500 pounds (8845 kg), including 2000 pounds (907 kg) of bombs or torpedoes carried under the wings. On production airplanes gross weight actually got as high as 23,386 lb (10,608 kg) while the ordnance payload increased to 4500 lb (2041 kg).

With war's end, the number of AM-I Maulers on order was reduced to 149 (bureau nos 22257/22355, 122388/122437), not including the prototypes. Early carrier qualification trials aboard USS *Kearsage* (CV-33) were successfully carried out by squadron VA-17A (later called VA-174) under LCDR G Wood, Jr, the Mauler being amenable to shipboard operations in part because of its large-area trailing-edge flaps which made for 'low and slow' flight in the pattern.

The Mauler went to sea with attack squadron VA-17A/VA-174 in March 1948, but shipboard operations did not last long and the type quickly reverted to shore duties with the Naval Air Reserve. Squadrons which operated the Mauler were VA-44, VA-45, VA-84, VA-85 and VA-176.

Martin delivered 17 of the 149 Maulers in AM-IQ

ABOVE LEFT
One company's Dauntless replacement, the Martin XBTM-1 Mauler in natural metal finish on 28 September 1945, probably at NAS Patuxent River, Maryland. Soon redesignated AM-1, the Mauler joined the Fleet only to serve briefly and not with much distinction (USN via R J Mills Jr)

LEFT
When the 'scout' mission was no longer needed in a Dauntless replacement, Douglas transformed the multiplace SB2D-1 Destroyer into the single-seat BTD-1, shown here and also called Destroyer. No one connected with the BTD-1 programme has anything favourable to say about the performance of the aircraft, seen from the beginning as being all wrong for the job (USN via R J Mills Jr)

TOP
Full-scale mockup of the XBT2D-1 Dauntless II aircraft, with large propeller spinner, is seen at Douglas' El Segundo plant on 18 August 1944. The outcome of the conflict remained uncertain and Navy planners expected to use the Dauntless II in the fight against Japan (MDC/Harry Gann)

configuration for electronic countermeasures (ECM) work. These carried a second crew member, an ECM operator, who boarded via a door on the starboard side of the fuselage. The AM-1Q airplanes were bureau nos 22296, 22346/22355, and 122388/122393. Some of these served with squadron VC-4 at NAS Atlantic City, New Jersey.

The AM-1 Mauler had a wing span of 50 ft 0 in (15.24 m), was 41 ft 2 in (12.55 m) long, and stood to a height of 16 ft 10 in (5.13 m). Wing area was 496 ft^2 (46.08 m^2).

Wags in the naval aviation community insisted that the letters in the AM-1 designation stood for 'awful monster'. One Patuxent Report on the Mauler was so distressing that it deserves to be quoted at length. The report recommended that '(1) the cockpit be completely redesigned; (2) unsatisfactory performance of flight instruments be corrected; (3) internal and external lighting be improved; (4) lateral trim control be improved at low speeds, and (5) provisions be made for more adequate cockpit ventilation.' Numerous other inadequacies were later found in the Mauler's design.

In a nutshell, the AM-1 Mauler was *heavy*. Pilots who could compare it with the AD-1 Skyraider—again, to get ahead of our story—found the Mauler not nearly manoeuvrable enough. Those whose only experience was with the unimpressive

SB2C Helldiver could find no fault with the Mauler except its weight.

Six and one-half years after qualifying for shipboard operation (in 1954), the AM-1 Mauler was to be seen only in the form of a relic stored on a barge at Norfolk, Virginia. *That* relic apparently was bureau no 122397, which was saved from an Army ordnance range to join the naval air museum at Pensacola, Florida. Thirty-two *more* years later, it is understood that the only two survivors are bureau no 22260 belonging to the Confederate Air Force (but yet to be restored or flown by them) and bureau no 22275 belonging to the Bradley Air Museum, Windsor Locks, Conn.

Douglas' New Design

On a trip to Washington, Douglas' key designer Edward Heinemann and his colleagues realized that if their firm was to get a major contract for a new warplane they were going to have to scrap the SB2D and BTD designs and come up with a wholly new aircraft. Given the long delays up to this point, the speed with which Heinemann turned everything around was nothing less than phenomenal.

It was June 1944 and Heinemann, Leo Devlin and Gene Root were ensconced in the Statler Hotel in Washington, DC—in town for what amounted to a showdown with the Navy. At this point the Mauler was only beginning to take shape at Martin's plant, the Kaiser BTK was the Navy's other likely candidate for a BT-class production order, and Heinemann had been told rather firmly that the Navy didn't see the BTD as a viable third choice. Martin or Kaiser building the Navy's vitally-needed BT? To the manufacturer of the Douglas Dauntless, the idea was unthinkable.

At a meeting with Navy officers, Heinemann offered to scrap the BTD design but insisted that Douglas was the best aircraft manufacturer to build a new BT. A little time, he insisted, would prove this conclusively. If the Navy would just give Heinemann's team thirty days to produce a new aircraft design, Heinemann argued forcefully, it would be a better aircraft than its competitors.

Rear Admiral Laurence B Richardson was sympathetic to the idea but not the time frame. 'Ed', he insisted, 'you'll have to have a [new] design for us by 0900 tomorrow'.

After a phone conversation with Donald Douglas in Santa Monica, Heinemann mustered Devlin and Root at the Statler; the trio set forth to devise a simple, sturdy, carrier-compatible torpedo/dive-bomber. Amid a pile of coffee cups, discarded sandwiches, notebooks and sheets of art paper, the trio laboured into the night, sketching, jotting down numbers, talking about dimensions. What size did a new BT have to be, to operate from *Essex*-class carriers? Should the proven R-2800 engine be used,

as Heinemann thought, or the bigger R-4360 favoured by Martin, or the newer and less proven R-3350? The men worked, talked, sipped coffee, drew pictures, and wrote down specifications.

At this time, Heinemann did not know what the new aircraft would be called, if, indeed, it ever came into existence at all. But the next Navy designation for a Douglas plane was BT2D and the name Dauntless II—evoking, as it did, the glory of Midway—sounded like a winner. Heinemann, Devlin and Root had absolutely no inkling they were designing the Douglas AD/A-1 Skyraider.

At this juncture, it would be fitting to have the skies open up while an archangel, or perhaps a tooth fairy, appears by magic to present Douglas a production order for the PDIAHR (Plane Designed In A Hotel Room). Heinemann could then be duly credited for his brilliance and the new warplane would live happily ever after. Or something.

But the new Douglas design was anything but the sudden heavyweight champion of a 1940s version of the *Rocky* fight films. The sky did not open up. The Navy did *not* see the light. As related earlier, the Martin design, the Mauler, was proceeded with.

What happened to the Douglas design was anything but dramatic. The Navy looked at it and said, well, maybe. Approval was given to proceed with the new design on the condition that a first flight be achieved within nine months. If that happened, the Navy promised that it would take another look and say . . . well, maybe . . .

Dauntless II

Pressured to have all engineering reports completed by January 1945 and to have a first flight by May,

TOP
One of two XBT2D-1N night attack aircraft, apparently at Mines Field (Los Angeles International Airport) on 18 February 1947. Evident from this angle is the squared-off top of the early Skyraider canopy screen. Later Skyraiders had a more rounded canopy shape (MDC/Harry Gann)

MIDDLE
XBT2D-1 Skyraider bureau number 09098, on 27 February 1948, probably at the newly-formed Naval Air Test Center (NATC), Patuxent River, Maryland. Although the BT2D-1 was redesignated AD-1 in April 1946, the earlier designation—XBT2D-1N for this variant—still appears in miniscule letters on the tail nearly two years later (USN via R J Mills Jr)

BOTTOM
XBT2D-1 Dauntless II bureau number 09089 ready for take-off. Douglas' Harry Gann, who knows more about his company's aircraft than anybody, says this machine later became an XBT2D-1N night attack aircraft. Another source indicates that airplanes 09098 and 09099 were the machines converted to XBT2D-1N standard (MDC/Harry Gann)

Final version of the Skyraider, the AD-7, was also the only airplane in the series never to be painted blue. Ship number 142010, the first AD-7 delivered to the Navy, basks in California sunshine (MDC/Harry Gann)

Heinemann's Douglas team moved ahead to create a warplane specified for a gross weight of 16,286 lb (7387 kg). Later this figure was changed to 16,120 lb (7311 kg). Considerable difficulty was encountered, as work proceeded, in sticking to the weight requirements. Delays were encountered. A mockup due for completion earlier was not completed until 1 August 1944 although, as will be seen (below), the Navy felt this was timely.

The aircraft was designated XBT2D. The first variant would be the XBT2D-1. The name Dauntless II was approved. The name seems, in fact, to be what was intended from the very beginning. The first fifteen XBT2D-1s were to be obtained from funds originally slated for the earlier BTD-1 under contract C-NOa(s)-743 of 31 August 1943. Amendment 16 to that contract, dated 21 July 1944, was written as a contract itself and superceded the earlier agreement. This amendment called for delivery of those BTD-1 airplanes which had not been cancelled (totalling 48, as of that time, plus the two jet-augmented BTD-2 airplanes) under 'Lot 1', and for 15 XBT2D-1 airplanes under 'Lot 2'.

An official report, written only a few months after the design period, describes the urgency of the situation:

This new dive-bomber was to be produced, like the [Kaiser Fleetwings] XBTK-1 and [Martin] XBTM-1 airplanes, on an expedited basis. The contractor, wishing to erase the unfavourable reaction to the model BTD-1 airplane, understood this desire for expediting the programme and showed it by building a very complete mockup in some 45 days. The mockup was held at the contractor's El Segundo plant in California from the 14th to the 17th of August, 1944. There were two mockups: (1) the mockup of the whole airplane was for the greater part rebuilt of metal and included a complete power plant installation [and] a complete cockpit (with an instrument panel incorporating red instrument lighting), [and] (2) a separate mockup of the cockpit only, made of wood, easy to modify, for the purpose of arriving at a final cockpit satisfactory to the [Navy] Board.

Heinemann's designers worked up a conventional, low-wing monoplane powered by the R-3350. Unusual fuselage dive-brakes were decided upon after other options were rejected: one would be located in the ventral position, the other two on each side of the fuselage between the wing and horizontal stabilizer. These 'barn doors' would provide plenty of drag without affecting wing lift, trim, or pilot control.

The very first Douglas XBT2D-1 Dauntless II (bureau number 09085) was rolled out in gleaming natural metal with red trim around the cowl and was a most impressive machine by the prevailing World War 2 standards. Although preceded by the Martin Mauler, the Douglas aircraft resulted from an almost compulsive attitude toward weight-saving and did not tip the scales overweight as the Martin design did. In fact, the first prototype actually came in 1800 lb (816 kg) below the manufacturers weight guarantee.

By the time it was readied for its first flight in the final days of World War 2, the Douglas machine was the result of thousands of man-hours of engineering effort and was an aircraft in which designers and the builder had enormous confidence.

Amendment 16 had specified a 'first flight' by June 1945, but Douglas was able to beat this deadline by a considerable margin. On 11 March 1945 at Mines Field (now Los Angeles International Airport), bureau number 09085 was ready for its first trip into the blue. Douglas test pilot LaVerne Browne, who had portrayed 'Tailspin Tommy' in a pre-war aviation movie, was chosen to make the maiden flight. The report quoted gives a contemporaneous description of pilot Brown's mount:

The XBT2D-1 was a single-seat, folding wing, high performance general purpose attack (dive-bomber and torpedo) airplane designed around the R-3350-34 engine (which later incorporated water injection). All stores were carried externally as no bomb-bay was provided. No displacing gear was used since Douglas Aircraft Co had designed, developed and manufactured a powder type bomb ejector which it was decided would be incorporated in the XBT2D-1 airplane. Bombs were carried on three stations (bomb ejector in fuselage centreline, one Mk 51 bomb rack in each wing, and 5-inch HVAR [high velocity aircraft rockets] on 8 stations (4 Mk 5-3 launchers on each outer wing panel)'.

Brown took off with the soon-to-be familiar roar of the eighteen-cylinder R-3350 engine—the report said the engine 'was still under development and its predecessor had given quite a bit of trouble'—and climbed over the airfield. The test pilot banked in the blinding sun over pre-smog Los Angeles and put the new airplane through a few routine manoeuvres. It was a remarkably successful 'first flight'. Although pilot Browne did not attempt anything dramatic, the BT2D-1 performed perfectly in his hands and no mechanical problems were encountered.

By 29 March 1945, airplane number one had completed no fewer than twenty flights. Dive brakes had been successfully tested at 300 mph (492 km/h). The aircraft had been flown with eight 5-inch rockets and with bombs weighing up to 2000 lb (907 kg). On 19 April 1945, during a dive, the engine failed but the airplane was close to Mines Field and landed safely. The engine and propeller were replaced and test flights resumed. Though the record is not clear on when the first BT2D-1 was transferred to NAS Patuxent River, Maryland, preliminary tests at the latter location were completed on 17 May 1945 on which date it was ferried back to Moffett Field.

No aircraft can enter service without some problems, and it would not be long before discovery of a structural flaw which caused wings to buckle when subjected to the pounding and slamming of carrier operations. But the BT2D-1 Dauntless II began its life with almost no hint of any design flaws. Almost from the outset, it was widely understood to be a better-performing aircraft than the competing Martin Mauler. Even so, the Navy was *still* saying only . . . well, maybe . . .

Wartime Planning

In March 1945, the war in Europe was approaching its end but no end to the Pacific conflict was in sight. No one really knew how the conflict with Japan could be resolved any time soon. In a new five-sided building in Washington called the Pentagon, military brass were preparing for Operation Olympic Coronet, the amphibious invasion of the Japanese home islands scheduled for early 1946. Even the handful of planners who knew about the Manhattan Project and its hush-hush effort to develop an atomic bomb had no idea when or whether the Project would succeed and could not have guessed that it would shorten the war. In this atmosphere, there was plenty of room to move ahead with a promising new naval aircraft. Almost immediately, Douglas was favoured with production orders for no fewer than 548 airframes.

Douglas received contracts for 25 BT2D-1 Dauntless II aircraft (bureau numbers 09085/09109). During the mockup inspection, it had been agreed that the first two of these would use the main shockstruts from Vought F4U Corsair airplanes, even though this would result in an understrength landing gear. Douglas was charged with putting full strength landing gear of its own design on the third and subsequent airplanes.

The manufacturer converted one of the first twenty-five machines (09096) to BT2D-1P photo-reconnaissance standard, the only dedicated recce bird in the entire history of the type. Two others (09098/09099) became BT2D-1N night operations aircraft while yet another (09109) became the sole XBT2D-1Q radar countermeasures aircraft.

The war with Japan ended on 15 August 1945, not so much because of the atomic bombs but because of the devastating effects of 'round-the-clock' B-29 Superfortress fire-bombing raids on Tokyo and other targets.

On that day, the United States possessed the biggest armada of military aircraft ever to exist on this planet. But just as quickly, the US disarmed. Hundreds of brand-new military aircraft were simply pushed over the side of carriers and buried at sea. Several aircraft types on order were simply cancelled altogether. The Douglas team fared better than many, although orders for the BT2D-1 were trimmed from 548 to 377, and soon thereafter to 277. It looked like more . . . well, maybe . . .

The second airplane (bureau no 09086) followed the first very closely and made its first flight on 8 May 1945. This machine was used for a flight vibration survey of the Eroproducts propeller in conjunction with the R-3350-8 engine (the R-3350-24) engines being not available in time to meet the initial flights of the first or second airplanes). In June 1945, this second machine was sent to the National Advisory Committee for Aeronautics (NACA) at NAS Moffett Field, California for full-scale wind-tunnel tests.

Douglas' rather ambitious static test programme suffered the same deceleration as the rest of the

LEFT
Two key figures in the Skyraider programme are designer Ed Heinemann (right) and Douglas test pilot LaVerne Brown, who made the first flight in the aircraft. The pair are seen in April 1952 beside another of their creations, the F3D-1 Skyknight fighter (MDC/Harry Gann)

ABOVE
Early AD-1 Skyraider in sea blue paint scheme and pre-947 national insignia flies over Los Angeles. Originally, the canopy was flat across the upper windshield brace. Later, a curved design was adopted (Douglas)

TOP
One of the great aviation photographers of the 1940s was Edgar Deigan of New Rochelle, New York, whose pictures illustrated books of the period. In this view, Deigan captures an AD-3 Skyraider, side number 403, taxying at an east coast airfield (Edgar Deigan)

programme after the surrender of Japan. Still, by mid-October 1945, all required primary structure static and dynamic load tests had been completed except for a few tests on the landing gear, engine mount, hoisting sling and ground loading devices. The Navy noted that the first fifteen airplanes (excepting bureau nos 09087 and 09089) had understrength catapult fittings whilst outer wing spar caps in all but three of the first fifteen airplanes were also understrength.

The third airplane (bureau no 09087) was out of the shop in May 1945 but, in July 1945, had to return to the factory for incorporation of full-strength catapulting and arresting provisions. Furthermore, due to the installation of very complete instrumentation to determine arresting and catapulting loads during platform tests at NAMC Philadelphia, the number three aircraft did not fly until 17 August 1945. It was moved to Philadelphia on 1 September 1945 and remained there for mock carrier weight tests.

Airplane number four (bureau no 09088) first flew on 6 October 1945. It had been allocated for demonstration purposes and the Navy agreed to Douglas's suggestion that it be stationed for a time at Palm Springs where the weather was consistently better than at El Segundo, although the aircraft returned to El Segundo in mid-November 1945.

BT2D-1 Dauntless II number five (bureau no 09089) as of 15 October 1945 had not yet flown but was scheduled to do so in December. The author, reflecting decades later on the difficulty of getting history right (did some pilot have a girlfriend in Palm Springs?) has not learned whether the date was met. Airplane number five was allocated to the manufacturer as a 'dog ship' to help Douglas to check installations, design changes and relocation of equipment.

Some of the early work on the powerplant, and on special versions of the BT2D, is interesting enough to

warrant further quotation from a document of the period, kindly supplied by Hal Andrews:

Alternate Power Plant:
At the beginning of the XBT2D-1 programme, it was decided that the contractor should investigate the use of an alternate powerplant, as insurance against the possibility that the R-3350-24 engine would not be developed to a satisfactory point.

The contractor was sent BuAer [US Navy Bureau of Aeronautics] Change Request Aer-E-12-JAT, serial 9906, dated 17 January 1945, for the study of a standby engine installation, in two model XBT2D-1 airplanes, of the Pratt & Whitney R-2800-34W engine. The contractor proceeded to study this installation and manufacture the necessary parts for its incorporation in two airplanes. However, as this study progressed, the R-3350-24 engine was developed (a two-speed clutch was finally designed which proved to be satisfactory) to a point where the standby installation had lost much of its reason for being. The contractor was therefore requested to cancel the actual installation of the R-2800-34W engine in two airplanes, but complete engineering and manufacture of parts and shelve them for future use should the need arise.

Gas Turbine Installation:
Recognizing the future role of gas turbines in aircraft, and in order to obtain a flying prototype dive-bomber with such an engine, the Bureau of Aeronautics sent to the contractor a Change Request . . . dated 16 April, 1945, asking for the installation of a TG-100 [jet] engine in one XBT2D-1 airplane. Two inspections of the mockup of this engine installation were made between 21 July and 17 August 1945. The contractor is to make the actual installation in XBT2D-1 airplane no 09097.

Spin-Stabilized Rockets:
The Bureau of Aeronautics sent to the contractor a Change Request . . . dated 12 April 1945 for the development of a spin-stabilized rocket attack version of the model XBT2D-1 airplane to carry internally, feed and fire in a single burst fifty or more 5-inch spin stabilized rockets. The contractor proceeded to study this new version and found that only about forty of these rockets could be internally carried in the wings. The contractor is now building a wing modified for this purpose, which will be ground tested at NOTS [Naval Ordnance Test Center] Inyokern, California. Later on an airplane will be flown with the modified wings, and air-firing tests will be conducted.

So far as can be determined, the gas turbine installation was not actually tested. The idea of providing some form of turbine power to the aircraft continued through its career, all the way up to the Vietnam era when Douglas proposed re-opening the factory lines for a gas-turbine powered version. BT2D-1 aircraft 09094 was modified with deletion of the standard pair of 20-mm cannons, these being replaced by a pair of tubes capable of firing 5-inch rockets. Each wing carried internally just six rounds of spin-stabilized rockets for ground attack (not 'only about forty' or 'fifty or more'). The system was tested at Inyokern 1946–48 but was never adopted.

Night Attack Study:
To provide two flying prototypes of a carrier-based night

attack version of the XBT2D-1 airplane, the contractor was asked . . . [on] 18 July, 1945 to study conversion of two airplanes to this new type. The night-attack version, officially designated as the XBT2D-1N airplane, is essentially to be the same as the basic airplane except that the main differences are:

(a) There are provisions in the aft fuselage for two men; one a radar operator and navigator, the other a radar countermeasures operator. These provisions include: seats, life raft, one exit door on each side of the fuselage.

(b) The fuselage brakes are deleted.

(c) Special electronics necessary to the mission of a night attack airplane.

The loading for this XBT2D-1N gave it a centre of gravity position which was aft of the design range. For this reason, NACA had been requested to determine aerodynamic and handling qualities of the XBT2D-1 airplane, buno 09086, at rearwards centre of gravity position.

A mockup of the night attack airplane was held at the contractor's plant on 15 and 16 October 1945 and was found acceptable . . .

In February 1946, the BT2D-1 was re-named Skyraider. Though it may have seemed inevitable to whoever thought of it, the Dauntless II name had never quite seemed right to most who encountered it. The Douglas company had manufactured a series of aircraft with the 'Sky-' prefix—indeed, the military version of the DC-3 was called the Skytrain—and it may have been wise, this decision not to perpetuate the name of its immortal predecessor. In more recent years, the success of Corsair II and Phantom II notwithstanding, attempts to re-use famous names have been, in general, diamal failures, witness the efforts of the misguided to dredge up Thunderbolt II for an aircraft which no one would ever compare to the original holder of the name.

Early XBT2D-1 Skyraider bureau number 09012 sat for many years in a blue paint scheme at NAS Oceana, Virginia as depicted on 14 September 1985. More recently, the aircraft was painted in grey, as seen on 23 April 1988 (William F Brabant)

Feline Flying

In April 1946, the Navy made adjustments in its designation system and the BT2D became the AD. 'Able Dog,' it would be called by thousands who flew it. The aircraft was now the beneficiary of a very ambitious development progamme with numerous airframes involved in test programmes and pre-service operations, so that it would have been perfectly apt to talk about the number of dog ships in the Able Dog programme. But one pilot uttered a cliché which evoked a different image from the animal world when queried about the handling characteristics of the new machine. Conveying a view that not all were destined to agree with, he said it performed 'with cat-like grace.'

So the new airplane came along too late to make a contribution to World War 2. The AD-1 Skyraider was about to enter service after the conclusion of a great war. Most Americans did not conceive that their young men would ever have to fight and most were preoccupied with the post-1945 boom in veterans' housing and college benefits, while they ignored the powerful armed forces they'd built up and allowed those forces to atrophy.

But it was not true, as some might have wanted to believe, that there would occur no further challenges to freedom. And a few brave men were willing to wear uniforms and fly airplanes for a living while everyone else was overdosing on the good life that had suddenly become available.

There was going to be some interesting post-war flying for those naval aviators fortunate enough to collar an assignment in the Skyraider. But the era of good feeling which came after VJ Day would not last forever and the Skyraider would not remain unblooded for long. Other wars lay ahead.

The time for 'well' and the time for 'maybe' had passed. The Douglas AD-1 Skyraider wouldn't help to defeat Nazi Germany or the Japanese Empire, but other challenges were soon to come.

Chapter 2
AD-2
The Skyraider
and the Guppy Shape

The first AD-1 Skyraiders were delivered to the Navy at Pacific Fleet Air Headquarters, NAS Alameda, California, located on the far side of the bay from San Francisco. Beautiful aeroplanes they were, adorned in the sea service's classic deep blue (glossy sea blue, or FS-595a colour 15042) paint scheme.

On the flight line, the Skyraiders were sharp and crisp in the sun that peeked through Bay Area clouds and fog, and post-war naval aviators, volunteers all, relished the mighty roar of the R-3350 engine and told themselves that this was what naval aviation was all about. Indeed, it seemed to be. A zealous young ensign buzzing Alameda at low level could take it all in from his open cockpit—the Fleet at anchor, the Bay Bridge looming out of the mist, mountains and forests in one direction, the Golden Gate and whitecapped crests of the Pacific in the other. That ocean was going to be important to Skyraider pilots: Americans seemed determined to get themselves into wars on the far side of it.

There must have been an ensign or two, and certainly more than a few plane captains—the stalwart crew chiefs who kept 'em flying—who noticed that among the glories of flying the Skyraider there were also some aggravations. The R-3350 churned up gouts of smoke and spewed leaks of oil everywhere. If not careful, you could break your neck tripping on an oil slick. The aircraft itself was a very solid design and a pleasure to maintain and fly, but there were teething troubles.

The cockpit was roomy and the pilot comfortable, but the original layout of the flight instruments and controls was far from ideal, and many improvements were to occur over a period of years before the layout was 'right'. As in any tail-dragger, the pilot had to S-taxi while moving his airplane on the ground, and even in the air visibility was not always perfect. The early Skyraiders were solid, able machines—'Able Dog' was a pilot's term for the aircraft, based on the

phonetics of the AD designation—but like a fine wine, the Skyraider was destined to improve with time and age.

In December 1946, attack squadron VA-19A at Alameda began to receive Skyraiders after structural changes had been made to cope with the problem of wing-buckling. East coast deliveries of the handsome blue Skyraider began in April 1947 when squadrons VA-3B and VA-3B received AD-1s and made their carrier qualification trials aboard USS *Sicily* (CVE-118).

Evaluation of the Skyraider at the newly-formed Naval Air Test Center (NATC) Patuxent River, Maryland, had produced minor changes in the production AD-1 Skyraider, including head and oxygen and additional lighting in the cockpit, as well as new lights in the aft compartment of the AD-1Q. Those tests were among the first performed for any US Navy aircraft type following the official founding of NATC in early 1946. The test centre, located in a scenic Maryland tidewater area close to the Chesapeake Bay, had at least one Skyraider on charge from the immediate post-war period until well into the 1950s.

Likewise, the Skyraider eventually found its way to Middle America, where there were no aircraft carriers but a few Naval Air Reserve units eager to operate the new type. It was still a rare sight in the 1940s but it became increasingly common to see a Skyraider touching down at NAS Glenview, Illinois or NAS Olathe, Kansas. It would not be an exaggeration to say that the hardy design of the Skyraider was apt for the people of the middle and far west of the country—who, in any event, often found themselves near some ocean and charged with fighting our wars.

The post-war years were lean ones for the Navy. Budget dollars were hard to come by, at a time when most Americans were interested in acquiring the

TOP
In what may be a previously unpublished view of post-war operations, LTJG M H Lax is at the controls on 30 June 1947 as AD-1 Skyraider bureau number 09199 catches the wire and plunks itself down upon the wooden deck of the carrier USS Tarawa *(CV-40) (USN, via Peter B Mersky)*

ABOVE
The Marine Corps took an early interest in Douglas' post-war attack aircraft. AD-2 Skyraider bureau number 122224, coded AK-11 and belonging to squadron VMA-121, banks in flight near MCAS El Toro, California in 1951 (Warren Bodie via Hal Andrews)

RIGHT
Typical formation of Skyraiders in blue over an equally blue ocean in the 1950s (USN via Peter B Mersky)

automobiles, houses and consumer goods unavailable to them during the long conflict. A rear admiral who'd spent his entire career hoping to command an aircraft carrier finally received his chance, but only if he would revert to captain immediately; he gladly surrendered his star for a rare billet at sea. There was less competition in the junior ranks—most of the eleven million Americans in uniform had quickly demobilized—but plenty of naval aviators wanted the chance to fly new aircraft. There was no lack of good men waiting to climb into the mighty Skyraider, turn over its sixteen and a half-foot propellers, and go leaping into the air in the big, powerful attack bomber.

Exciting Aircraft

It was exciting to crank up the huge, smoke-belching R-3350 and go off on a hop—flying under the Golden Gate Bridge as one ensign reportedly did, or buzzing the tower at North Island from an altitude of twenty feet while carrying a full ordnance load. A few jet aircraft were beginning to appear, the forgettable McDonnell FH-1 Phantom and North American FJ-1 Fury among them, but in the post-war years the big 'Able Dog' was about the most impressive naval warplane a man could fly.

In 1947, the Navy decided it wanted an additional 151 Skyraiders, a figure which soon rose to 194 and then to 269. The AD-1Q radar countermeasures Skyraider, what was known in those days as a radar picket ship and would be called an ECM (electronic countermeasures) aircraft today, was proving suc-

LEFT
Some Skyraiders belonged not to attack squadrons but to fighter units. This one, assigned to VF-54 and piloted by LCDR W H Alexander is cracking up aboard Korean War veteran USS Philippine Sea (CVA-47) on 12 June 1954 (USN via Peter B Mersky)

ABOVE
Unfortunately, a Korean War-era censor got ahold of this superb view of five AD-1 Skyraiders in flight and 'blacked out' tail codes and unit information. Date of the photo is 17 October 1952 (USN via Peter B Mersky)

cessful. The radio countermeasures operator in the rear compartment of the AD-1Q (an enlisted sailor) had to be almost a scientist. He was equipped with AN/APR-1 search receiver, AN/APA-11 pulse analyser, AN/APA-38 panoramic adapter, and MX-346/A window dispenser. The AD-1Q could carry AN/APS-4 radar pod under the right wing. With its distinctive ECM blister on the lower rear fuselage, fed by an airscoop aft of the radio mast, as well as other bulges and antennas—one identifying feature was the ECM compartment door on the port fuselage—the AD-1Q became a familiar sight at naval air stations and in the fleet.

Structural problems continued to plague the AD-1 and AD-1Q Skyraiders, however. Slamming a heavy prop airplane down on a carrier deck was not always good for a pilot's digestion and it was rarely anything but sheer brutality for the airframe. Sturdy-looking, yet designed with meticulous attention to weight, the Skyraider simply wasn't strong enough.

In the new AD-2 version, the inner structure of the wing was strengthened and other changes were made for the purpose of rendering the Skyraider amenable to being thumped down on a carrier deck. Remarkably, these changes were made without endangering the Skyraider's charter membership in the Weight Watchers Club.

Still, the AD-2, first delivered to the Fleet in early 1948, was a vastly improved and far more powerful Skyraider. Powerplant was the improved R-3350-26W, capable of 3020 hp at take-off. Exhaust pipes and the exhaust collector ring were revised. An external fuel tank was added for the first time, increasing fuel capacity by some 500 gallons.

The AD-2 also introduced a revised and more comfortable pilot's headrest, a very interesting change in the layout of the cockpit controls (a small flap representing the flaps, a small wheel for the wheels, and so on), and hinged undercarriage doors. These were all interim changes and were implemented without any major delays in the flow of the El Segundo production line.

With increased fuel capacity and greater range—able, now, to fly an attack mission out to a radius of 600 miles (965 km), loiter overhead for twelve minutes, and return—the AD-2 Skyraider retained the twin 20-mm cannons of earlier aircraft but had two additional wing racks for bombs or rockets. The basic design remained unchanged despite these additions to the load that had to be carried under combat conditions. 156 AD-2s were delivered to the Navy, along with 21 AD-2Q radar countermeasures aircraft (with a radar operator buried in the fuselage below and behind the pilot). Also employed by the Navy during this period was the sole AD-2QU (bureau no 122373) which functioned as a target-towing aircraft.

Marine Machine

The AD-2 was also delivered to the US Marine Corps, which became an enthusiastic user of early Skyraiders. AD-2s served with Navy VA (attack), VF (fighter), VC (composite) and Marine VMA (attack) squadrons. The 'Night Hawks' of VC-33 at NAS Norfolk, Virginia employed the AD-2Q variant from 1949.

Lieutenant (jg) Jerry F Hoganson began his naval aviation career in the post-war years with basic flight training in the North American SNJ and progressed to advanced flying in the F4U-4 Corsair. He was always fond of the gull-winged Corsair but in February 1950 his squadron converted from the F4U-4 to the AD-2 Skyraider and Hoganson immediately fell in love with the new airplane.

In training exercises in the Caribbean, Hoganson

found the Skyraider easy to handle, comfortable to fly, and relatively forgiving so long as the pilot never forgot the massive torque forces at work on the airplane.

'It was an honest airplane,' says Hoganson who is today a retired commander and programme manager for an aerospace firm. 'It didn't get into a spin at low speeds the way the F4U did. It was a stable airplane, a good gun platform.' It was possible to raise the seat, a feature which helped considerably though some S-taxying was still required on the ground. 'If it was trimmed and flown right, there was no better machine to deliver a bomb or rocket.' Hoganson found that the guns were prone to jamming, a problem which was to persist throughout the Skyraider's lifetime.

In comparing his two aircraft types, Hoganson remembered that the AD-2 had better visibility than the F4U-4. In the Corsair, you needed muscles and a hand crank to close the canopy, while the Skyraider had 3000-lb (1360 kg) hydraulic pressure. This was important because, although Skyraider pilots initially kept the hood open for take-offs and landings, they soon learned as a safety precaution to land on a carrier with the canopy closed: they could hear better. This did not, of course, prevent a few diehards from doing it the old way and the Navy had to remind everybody that at low speed with an open cockpit, fumes were a danger.

AD-3 Variant

It had long been obvious that, apart from its attack role, the Skyraider had promise for a variety of other missions. The AD-3 series finally demonstrated this. At one time, the third variant was supposed to carry either a Douglas-designed twin turbine, twin Allison 500s, or a Westinghouse 24-C and 19XB. However, the gas turbine-powered Skyraider programme quickly gained so much momentum that it became a separate aircraft type, the A2D-1 Skyshark. The AD-3 came into the world as a very conventional improvement over the -1 and -2 variants.

The Navy eventually acquired 125 AD-3s, 23 AD-3Qs (originally ordered as AD-3QU target tugs), 31 AD-3W early-warning aircraft and 15 AD-3Ns designed for night operations. Two airplanes were converted from AD-3W to AD-3E standard as 'hunters' with special anti-submarine electronics equipment, while two other machines were converted from AD-3N to AD-3S to team up as 'killers.' The notion of employing a two-ship 'hunter/killer' team to stalk and wipe out the Russians' dreaded submarines will shortly reappear in this narrative.

AD-4 Skyraider 123798, a Korean War veteran belonging to Carrier Air Group Three, operates aboard USS Franklin D Roosevelt (CVA-42) during a readiness inspection on 17 March 1953 (USN via Harold Andrews)

TOP LEFT
*Naval Air Development AD-1 Skyraider in flight in the
early 1950s (USN via Peter B Mersky)*

ABOVE
*Classified CONFIDENTIAL at the time it was taken and
later released, this view of Naval Air Test Unit AD-2
Skyraider 122355 shows release of an aerial torpedo
similar to those employed in combat in the Korean War
(USN via Peter B Mersky)*

Sea blue Skyraiders on the line at the Douglas plant in El Segundo on 14 September 1953. These are late-model AD-6s, the final variant delivered in blue paint (Douglas)

Douglas AD-2 Skyraider extends the under-fuselage dive brake on an early developmental flight, 27 October 1949. The dive brake remained a standard feature of the attack bomber, although in Vietnam the brake was frequently wired shut to permit use of a centreline fuel tank (Douglas via Harold Andrews)

In the AD-3 version, the main landing gear oleo stroke was lengthened by 14 inches. The main gear thus had greater 'flex' and load-bearing capacity. A new shape was created for the tail wheel which was no longer fully retractable. The discerning modeller on the alert for every change will detect a hand hold located near the tail wheel to make moving the aircraft on the ground (or on a carrier deck) more manageable.

Other improvements with the AD-3 version included significant changes in the cockpit instrument layout, these being based on recommendations from the Fleet to make the pilot's job easier. Years before the acronym MMI (machine-man interface), the AD-3 was created with concern for the 'ergonomy' (man-efficiency) of its instruments and flight controls. Also on the AD-3, the pitot tube which had been added to the vertical fin of the AD-2 was deleted.

The AD-4 followed in the late 1940s, outwardly little different from other Skyraiders but with internal structural improvements and a significant increase in gross weight from 18,500 lb (8392 kg) to 24,000 lb (10,886 kg). A sturdier and heavier machine meant, at last, a decisive end to the carrier operation problems which had beset the Skyraider earlier in its career. It could be said that with the '-4' model, the definitive Skyraider was finally decided upon.

In one of those incidents told and re-told when naval aviators convene at the bar, on AD-4 pilot launched from NAS Miami, Florida (now the Coast Guard's Opa Locka base), climbed away, and headed northwest on a cross-country flight. A serious mechanical problem—details no longer remembered—made it necessary for the pilot to leave his AD-4 in mid-air some 50 miles (80 km) northwest of the base.

The pilot must have been over the Everglades swamp when he hit the silk, for it took three days before rescuers found him safe and sound. The fate of his aircraft was immediately known to all, however:

ABOVE
Douglas AD-2Q 122366 sitting on the hardstand compass rose at El Segundo on 8 September 1948 (Douglas via Harold Andrews)

RIGHT
LTJG Charles C Carte had a bad day on 20 January 1954 when he made this not-so-good landing aboard USS Yorktown *(CVS-10) (USN via Harold Andrews)*

The erstwhile AD-4 made a gentle 180-degree bank which put it on a southeast heading going straight back to NAS Miami, made a gradual letdown toward the airfield as if a glide slope had been pre-determined, and plunked itself down between two Miami hangars. A witness reportedly wondered if some invisible ghost were sitting in the open cockpit. Unfortunately, it was not a perfect landing, however: the aircraft and both hangars were engulfed in the ensuing blaze.

Not every story from the era involved such devastation. At a California naval air station, a group of Skyraider pilots staged a mock 'air war' for the benefit of a local charity. Hellcats and Corsairs tangled with each other and strafed. Skyraiders came in and dropped ordnance. The Saturday afternoon event raised hundreds of thousands of dollars in charitable contributions.

Though it had not been specified as an improve-ment, pilots found that the AD-4 could operate at higher altitudes. One document from the period lists a service ceiling for earlier Skyraiders of 28,500 ft (8685 m) and indicates that the AD-4 could get considerably higher.

In fact, it appears that the AD-4 could get up to 39,450 ft (12,024 m), and some importance was attached to its ability to operate at great altitude where Air Force bombers flew.

Radar Gear

A major improvement with the AD-4 was the APS-19A radar which required a revised instrument panel with a Mod 3 or Mod 4 bomb director. The aircraft also carried a modified P-1 autopilot. There were

ABOVE
AD-3 Skyraider of El Segundo, 24 September 1948 (Douglas via Harold Andrews)

RIGHT
Skyraider (09286, 123771) tested at the Naval Air Test Center, Patuxent River, Maryland, in the 1950s (USN)

minor changes in the AD-4 windscreen to improve bullet-proofing and a distinctive recognition feature was added in the form of a pitot tube projecting forward from the top of the vertical tail's leading edge. A total of 372 airframes in the AD-4 series were delivered, with some plans for additional purchases being cancelled during the lean budget years of the 1940s.

Included in that number were 28 aircraft converted to AD-4B standard, introducing the definitive armament of four 20-mm cannons and being equipped for what the Navy calls 'special munitions'—that is, atomic bombs. A further 165 AD-4B aircraft were delivered from the factory, although 14 more were cancelled during one of several contract reviews.

The capability to carry a nuclear weapon was all-important to the Navy's plans. In a gruelling Capitol Hill inquiry in 1948, the Congress came to the reluctant conclusion that the Air Force's B-36 bomber was the best weapon for the money in the fast-growing strategic confrontation with Moscow. The Navy had sought without success to 'sell' legislators on the proposed super carrier USS *United States* (CVA-58) but the carrier was eventually cancelled while generals and admirals in the Pentagon struggled to get the best of each other in the fierce competition for very scarce budget dollars.

In the shameless inter-service rivalry of the late 1940s, 'carrier admirals' were determined to convince Congress that there was a need for the Fleet's carrier force, while 'bomber generals' argued that sparse budget dollars should be spent instead on even more B-36, and later B-47, bombers. Lobbying efforts, Capitol Hill testimony, and even some arm-twisting went into the admirals' efforts to convince legislators to authorize a new generation of carriers. Any senator or representative who had the yen to *visit* an aircraft carrier was likely to be given the Red Carpet Tour, replete with gourmet dinner at the captain's mess— without alcohol, of course, because American warships are dry.

Since there had to be a reason for carriers, the admirals invented a mission—delivering atomic bombs to the Commie Hordes in the Soviet Union, who revealed their own colours by exploding *their* first atomic bomb in 1949. In those post-war years, a number of brave naval aviators struggled to operate P2V-3 Neptunes from carrier decks and later grappled with the ungainly AJ-1 Savage, all to give the Fleet a nuclear mission. Eventually it was going to be 'one-man control' of the dreaded Nuke, with the Big Bomb being entrusted to the single pilot of a single-seat aircraft.

Domesday Weapon

In his superb appreciation *Skyraider: The Douglas A-1 'Flying Dump Truck'*, (Annapolis: Nautical & Aviation Press, 1982) veteran Skyraider pilot Captain Rosario (Zip) Rausa reveals that ship number 123805 (an AD-4) became the first single-engine aircraft to carry a simulated atomic weapon. Ed Heinemann's group designed installation requirements with the able help of R G Smith who, in addition to having a major design role on the Skyraider, is also one of the world's great aviation artists.

Though tests were conducted with a 'shape'—the jargon for a dummy bomb—it is not thought that any Skyraider ever carried an actual atomtic weapon.

Certainly, no AD-4B Skyraider ever actually dropped an atomic bomb (the term was in wide use

then; nuclear weapon was not), not even during the frequent atmosphere tests that took place in the western Pacific. It remains very doubtful that any Skyraider even *carried* an atomic bomb on an actual flight and, certainly, members of carrier-based attack squadrons did not see employing The Nuke as a real event that was likely to happen to them. This did not prevent the admirals from beseeching Congress to buy carriers instead of B-36s. A map prepared for the legislators showed how carrier-based aircraft could pulverize hundreds of targets in the Soviet Union—though one legislator wondered how, on this fanciful map, the Navy had gotten its carriers into the Baltic, the Black Sea and the Caspian Sea!

To speak further of models in the AD-4 series, some 307 additional airplanes were delivered as the AD-4N, being equipped with the new radar for night operations. The US Navy had no other night-capable combat aircraft operating from shipboard at this time. Of these machines, 100 were later converted to AD-4NA with some equipment removed to 'strip' the aircraft for the attack role. 37 more were converted to AD-4NL, being winterized for operations in arctic weather with the addition of wing leading-edge de-icer boots and other minor improvements.

Sub-Hunter

To thousands of men who maintained and flew her in that capacity, the AD Skyraider will be remembered as an anti-submarine aircraft. It hardly seems possible in the present day, but in the 1940s Americans were afflicted by a paranoia about the USSR's underwater fleet, built up dramatically by the Soviets after exploiting wartime German tech-

nology. Articles in newspapers and news magazines (and stories on that new medium, television) warned that communist domination of the world was being rapidly advanced by the expansion of Moscow's submarine armada.

Anti-submarine aircraft, whether based on land or aboard carriers (including a new class, the anti-submarine carrier or CVS, to which ageing vessels like *Randolph* and *Intrepid* were converted) seemed increasingly to be of vital importance to the US and its allies as the number of Soviet submarines reached 350, then 400, then 450. Present-day submarine-launched ballistic missiles (SLBMs), which can attack US targets with a warning time of less than a minute, were still very much in the future, but submarines were seen as posing a grave threat to the US Navy's surface fleet.

The Navy had been doing considerable work in developing additional roles for the Skyraider at the very time anti-submarine weaponry ranked second only to new carriers on the admirals' shopping lists.

In March 1949, the Navy's Bureau of Aeronautics examined mockups of proposed AD-4S (search) and AD-4E (attack) versions of the Skyraider, to team up as 'hunter' and 'killer' in the Fleet's continuing contest with the Soviet Union's expanding submarine force. A similar 'hunter/killer' mission against submarines was carried out by the Navy's

Grumman AF-2 Guardian aircraft with some success. Flight tests at Patuxent with AD-3S and AD-3E Skyraiders led to changes in an ongoing purchase contract for airplanes in the AD-4 series, modifying 81 machines on the production line for the 'hunter/killer' mission.

The Navy wanted additional 'hunter/killer' Skyraiders. It soon became apparent, however, that with the capabilities of the new AN/APS-31 radar carried by the search airplanes, a single aircraft could perform both roles. The new radar offered a 28-inch scanner screen which could be contained within a 36-inch housing. Douglas had produced the radar at five per cent below projected costs and was now ready to propose a new 'hunter/killer,' in one airframe, to be known as the AD-5. As it evolved over time, the AD-5 was to possess a totally redesigned crew area, with side-by-side seating for the first time. Navy planners shelved the project, however, when other needs took priority.

AD versus B-36

Most naval aviators who took the AD Skyraiders to sea in the late 1940s were intent on improving their assigned mission—ground attack. Air-to-air combat, the 'fighter business,' was pretty much left to those squadrons which operated the F4U Corsair or F8F Bearcat. This may have been a mistake: although no serious training in air-to-air tactics was *ever* conducted in the Skyraider community, Ed Heinemann's versatile aircraft was destined to repeatedly disprove those who insisted that it could not be used as a fighter.

Mixed formations, known to a later generation as Alpha Strikes, were far from unusual and a brace of Corsairs might escort a flight of Skyraiders on a typical raid against a simulated enemy. Combat missions were hi-hi-lo in those days, at least much of the time, and at a conservative cruising altitude a Skyraider force could easily strike a target 500 miles (804 km) away and return safely to the carrier. The fighter cover would prevent the bad guys from intervening.

AD-4N Skyraider 127854 (foreground) follows companions into the break on 13 March 1953 during flight operations from NAS Moffett Field south of San Francisco. Exact colour or purpose of underwing panels, which are not standard Navy blue, are not known (USN via Peter B Mersky)

It continued to rankle the admirals that Capitol Hill budget money was going into the Strategic Air Command's B-36 and B-47 bombers, and on more than one occasion Naval Air people tried to find a way to 'show up' SAC.

The 'Warhorses' of attack squadron VA-55 under LCDR N D Hodson were located on the west coast in 1949 and were directed to intercept SAC B-36s approaching from offshore and 'do something' to demonstrate the superiority of the carrier-based aircraft. It is unclear whether this exercise could have

caused much concern for Soviet Tupolev Tu-4 bomber crews: there were those who suggested that the Navy was more interested in outwitting the Air Force than in defeating the Russians!

Lieutenant (jg) Fredric B Newman was a member of VA-55 and remembers how the Skyraider pilots strained their way aloft from NAS North Island, California, to go out to sea and chase after the B-36. Newman had flown the twin-Beech SNB ('Slow Navy Bomber,' many called it) and the Grumman TBF Avenger, so the Skyraider was by far the best-performing airplane he'd ever piloted. 'Still, it was one heck of a strain for us to get up there. We were supposed to intercept the B-36s at around 35,000 feet [10,668 m], *and make it look easy*, but it wasn't all that easy. In fact, that was about as high as we could fly. So although we took some photos to illustrate our 'superiority' over the Air Force, most of us never forgot that our real job was ground attack'.

make its approach in the nose-high attitude, which was perfectly okay for the pilot except that you had one hell of a visibility problem. So I learned how to line myself up on the incomplete pylons for the bridge and use them as a guide—it worked on the same principle as a primitive bombsight, just align yourself between two points—and after some practice I could bring her in perfectly. After the bridge was completed, the road went over the pylons so this method didn't work any more.' The bridge Newman is talking about is not very high, and it's a safe bet that no Skyraider pilot ever flew *under* this particular span!

'Guppy'

The ability of the Skyraider to carry almost anything is one theme which will recur in this volume. It seemed that if you wanted to hang an extra item of equipment on the Skyraider, all you needed to do was to create a new bump or bulge. There is no sign that aerodynamic drag was ever a problem in an aircraft described by one pilot as 'already having the flight characteristics of a barn door' and certainly weight-carrying was almost never a problem for the aeroplane. So it was inevitable that a few special versions of the Skyraider would acquire the swollen belly appendage which caused these variants to become known as 'guppy' airplanes.

To continue the alphabet soup of AD-4 sub-variants, the AD-4W was a three-place Skyraider with the now-familiar 'guppy' radar installation for airborne early warning (AEW). No fewer than 168 were manufactured. Fifty of these were transferred to the Royal Navy and operated as the Skyraider AEW.1, initially with No 778 Sqn, Fleet Air Arm, beginning in 1951.

British Skyraiders

The first four Skyraider AEW.1s provided to the United Kingdom under the Mutual Defense Assistance Pact (MDAP) crossed the Atlantic slowly, arriving in Glasgow on 9 November 1951 aboard the merchantman SS *American Clipper*. (In chapter four, the full story of the 'foreign' Skyraider will be related, but a brief synopsis appears here for continuity).

No 778 Sqn had been formed the previous month to evaluate American electronics equipment. Redesignated No 849 Sqn on 7 July 1952, this Royal Navy unit eventually operated four flights of AEW Skyraiders and carried out the warning function until the Fairey Gannet could be developed.

No 849 Sqn, whose first skipper was LCDR J D Treacher, operated the glossy sea blue Skyraiders from Culdrose for almost a decade before the airplanes were gradually deleted from service in February 1960. Never easy to fly from carrier decks,

Fred Newman, a retired commander and Washington consultant, remembers that the flying-time allotments were slashed in the budget-lean late 1940s, and pilots competed fiercely with each other for hours in the Skyraider, 'One favourite trip was the cross-country from Pensacola to the old Anacostia naval air station in Washington, DC. Washington is a beautiful town and there were periodic requirements for somebody to fly up there hauling documents. We loved to RON [rest overnight] there, and the trip was usually good for about a dozen extra hours of flying time.'

Newman remembers when construction was under way for the South Capitol Street Bridge across the Potomac River about 1,000 ft (305 m) from the end of the runway at Anacostia. 'Although you were supposed to bring it down in a level attitude and allow it to settle on the tailwheel only after reaching the ground, the AD Skyraider always seemed to 'want' to

they were much-loved nonetheless, although their bulbous, under-fuselage radar housings were the inevitable grist for jokes about pregnancy, kangaroos and basketballs. These erstwhile Skyraiders (and their Gannet successors) provided exactly the much-needed early-warning capability which Britain's carrier force found itself lacking during the later, 1982 Falklands conflict.

From this contingent of 'foreign Skyraiders,' some 14 airframes were later transferred to Sweden, and 'civilianized' with 'guppy' radar deleted to serve as civil-registered target tows. The removal of that distinctive bulge under the belly restored the airplanes to the functional gracefulness that was so much a part of the basic design. Painted a brilliant yellow and given Swedish civil registry numbers, the

TOP LEFT
AD-2 Skyraider makes a low-level pass at NATC Patuxent River, Maryland in the early 1950s (USN)

FAR LEFT AND ABOVE
Taken near NATC Patuxent River, Maryland in the early 1950s, these views of AD-2 Skyraider 122300 show a varied ordnance load which is, in fact, too much ordnance to carry very far! On the centreline is a Mark 13 torpedo of the kind that would soon be needed halfway around the world (USN)

airplanes were a familiar sight at Stockholm's Bromma Airport well into the 1980s. In due course, they were replaced in their target tow duties by the Mitsubishi Mu-2.

At least two of the Swedish-registered Skyraiders later found their way back to Great Britain, where, in 1985, they were stored at North Weald, awaiting a new owner's plans to transform them into airshow warbirds. Bob Collins, an American businessman in London, led the author up to North Weald for an inspection, having decided that he would like to purchase a Skyraider that he and wife Maureen could fly around in (he may have done so, by this time). The aircraft were then in somewhat forlorn-appearing condition but it required little imagination to hear the R-3350 turning over and to see the Skyraiders churning through the air once again. In looking over these very old AD-4W aeroplanes, one was reminded again—the point cannot be stressed too often—how sturdy the Skyraider is.

The disposition of former Royal Navy Skyraiders runs considerably ahead of the rest of the story. As the 1950s began, the Skyraider was comfortably settled in US service, albeit with production orders not coming in as fast as Douglas might have liked. Gradually, the Navy and Marine Corps were acquiring a skilled cadre of men who would bulwark the Fleet's medium attack squadrons and spend much of their career in the Douglas aeroplane.

Don McNicholl went into the Skyraider after completing flight training in early 1950. Although part of the active-duty Navy, Don was sent to serve with a Naval Air Reserve unit in the midwest. 'They had just gotten some AD-2s from the Fleet and were operating a relatively new airplane for the first time. They were a spunky bunch and not all of them followed the regulations in every detail.' Don's unit and location are not named here to protect the guilty.

'We had this Skyraider jock whom I'll call Red Hot Harry. He was a very young JG [lieutenant, junior grade] and he was dating a nurse from the air station's dispensary. Red Hot Harry immediately had the idea that the nurse would appreciate him better if she could share his experience of flying in a blue AD-2.

'With a full load of ammo for the 20-mm cannons, Harry took off one day with this nurse sitting in a kind of sidesaddle position in his lap in the Skyraider's cockpit. It was roomy in there, but not *that* roomy. Later on, he told all of us that he didn't have visibility worth a damn but that, "it sure felt good."

'We had permission to use an abandoned quarry for target practice on an individual basis. After confirming the proper clearance to do so, Red Hot Harry flew over there with the nurse in his lap. Somehow, Harry managed to find the quarry and make a clearing turn. Apparently the nurse helped him to charge the guns. Red Hot Harry made several diving passes at the target, fired all of the Skyraider's ammunition, and returned to our base with Zero

Damage to himself, his airplane, or his girlfriend. PS, a year or so Harry married a different woman and remains married to her to this day.

My own experiences were far more modest,' McNicholl continues. 'I do know that there was a tendency on the part of some of the guys to make low-speed buzzing passes over picnic grounds, school yards and other places. There was also some pretty fierce competition for the cross-country slots on the schedule, with each guy in the squadron wanting to visit somebody at a choice location a few hundred miles away.

'All I can say is, we enjoyed flying that airplane. Many of us had been too young for World War 2 and to be honest we never thought a whole lot about war as a real thing. After all, we had just recently been victorious over the bad guys and it hardly seemed likely that we would have to fight again. There was always conversation about the Russians, but . . .'

Interlude's End

In many ways, those years 1945–50 were an interlude. The newly independent Air Force and the Navy were testing some dramatically new and different aircraft—jet engines, swept-back wings, even flying wings—while continuing to depend on very conventional, piston-engine warplanes for their contingency needs. A generation of young men were supremely confident in their uniforms, units and airplanes. Training was not especially realistic, not in Skyraider squadrons and not anywhere else. War plans existed in Washington's Main Navy building and in the new Pentagon, but those plans rarely filtered down to the squadrons in any form that was understood by the men.

It was certainly true that the Skyraider was, up to this point, a 'peacetime' airplane. The American attitude toward armed conflict was almost innocent in its presumption that if any fighting did erupt anywhere, the good guys would quickly dispense with the foreign aggressors.

Commander Hodson's VA-55 was aboard USS *Valley Forge* (CVA-45) on a western Pacific cruise when 25 June 1950 arrived. The day began with no flying activities and routine operations aboard the ship, which was at that time not far from Hong Kong. Before long, people were listening to the radio and talking about developments that were taking place not far away. There were reports that the President, Harry S Truman, who had secured re-election eighteen months earlier by only the narrowest of margins, was convening some unusual meetings.

A squadron member recalls that several pilots were lounging in the ready room when an officer burst in and told everybody to stop goofing off. 'And somebody take a good look at our map situation, will you?' the officer sounded impatient. 'We're going to need a whole bunch of maps of Korea.'

Chapter 3
AD-3
The Skyraider
in a Porcine Setting

'There are only three things the soldiers in Japan are afraid of,' Colonel Harry G Summers, Jr was told by his commander when he arrived in Seoul in 1947. 'That's gonorrhea, diarrhea and Korea . . . and you've got the last one.' The Asian peninsula has a very positive image in the world today, but in an earlier era Summers' quote is apt. It was even more apt after 25 June 1950 when Skyraider squadrons went to war there.

North Korea's portly Kim Il Sung, not a very deserving figure to hold the distinction of longest-surviving head of state in our times, made a heinous miscalculation.

Kim believed, with some cause, that Americans—lulled by the good life in the post-war years—were too somnolent to come to the aid of a friendly but obscure country on his peninsula, a country which

Secretary of State Dean Acheson had appeared to dismiss as inconsequential in a 1949 speech. Kim's armies poured across the 38th Parallel in the early hours of 25 June 1950, spearheaded by columns of Soviet-built T-34 tanks, bent on achieving a lightning victory and unifying Korea under the hammer and sickle.

President Harry S Truman immediately took the decision Kim had thought him not courageous enough to take. Truman ordered United States forces to the defence of South Korea and took steps which brought sixteen United Nations countries into the conflict. USS *Valley Forge*, (CVA-45) with Carrier Air Group Five (Skyraiders included), pulled anchor in Hong Kong and sailed for Korean waters.

The Douglas AD Skyraider, now in its third and fourth major versions (AD-3 and AD-4), was by now

A waveoff from the landing signal officer (LSO) is an order to 'go around' and make another attempt before landing on the carrier. In October 1952, this AD-1 Skyraider returning from a strike over Korea has just been waved off and is making the requisite go-around. Some pilots found the risks involved in landing on carriers to be as great as those of combat. Ship seen here is USS Bon Homme Richard *(CVA-31) (USN)*

ABOVE
The AD Skyraider and F4U Corsair were the two principal US Navy 'prop jobs' of the Korean War. Both also scored air-to-air kills. One Corsair pilot shot down MiG-15 and another became an ace by downing five 'Bedcheck Charlie' nocturnal intruders. A Marine Corps AD-4NL Skyraider crew were credited with shooting down a North Korean Po-2 biplane (via Peter Mersky)

TOP RIGHT
AD-1 Skyraider, laden with bombs on ordnance stations outboard of the wing fold, taxies toward launch on the wooden deck of USS Princeton *(CV-37) off Korea. AD-1 through AD-4 models were used throughout the 1950–53 Korean War (via Dave Ostrowski)*

RIGHT
Its own tail hidden behind the wing cannons of a fellow 'dash four' model, AD-4NL Skyraider 124757 is seen at Chanute Field, Illinois in 1951 (via Paul D Stevens)

ABOVE
USS Valley Forge *was at anchor in Hong Kong when the Korean War broke out and rushed quickly to the scene of the fighting. Here, 'Happy Valley's' straight deck is filled with F9F Panthers and AD Skyraiders painted in Navy blue (USN)*

RIGHT
An AD-4W Skyraider, belly radar easily visible, has tailhook lowered on approach to USS Coral Sea *(CVB-43) in the Mediterranean Sea on 6 November 1950 (via Paul D Stevens)*

embarked on just about every one of the US Navy's veteran, straight-back aircraft carriers. The Skyraider was serving, as well, with the Marine Corps.

In Korea, the first combat missions were flown by US Air Force F-80 Shooting Stars, F-82 Twin Mustangs and B-26 Invaders operating from Japanese bases, but the Navy's carrier air groups quickly joined the fray as did Marine Corps aviation. The Skyraider's range, loitering time, ordnance-carrying capacity, and ability to sustain punishment, were put to the test. So, too, as seasons changed, was the Skyraider's ability to function in a gruelling winter environment.

It was, of course, still summer when the first naval air strikes were flown against onrushing North Korean forces on 3 July 1950. While jets hit Haeju airfield 60 miles (93 km) farther north, a flight of twelve Skyraiders struck at the capital, Pyongyang. Anti-aircraft fire was heavy and the naval warplanes tangled briefly with North Korean Yak-3 and Yak-9 prop-driven fighters.

It is a pity that no one carried a camera during this mission. It is easy to imagine a painting of the scene— the enemy's largest city sprawled in the background, smoke rising from bomb hits, a Skyraider turning in a hard bank, its wings vertical to the ground as its pilot struggles in vain to outmanoeuvre a Yak. Through out the duration of this air battle, puffs of black smoke from the enemy's anti-aircraft fire were everywhere.

One VA-55 Skyraider was hit by a 37-mm shell which damaged its hydraulics and make it necessary for the pilot to attempt a fast landing, without flaps, aboard *Valley Forge*. The Skyraider bounded over crash wires laid across the deck, slammed into other aircraft and wrecked itself and two Corsairs while damaging a half-dozen other aircraft. It was the first of repeated illustrations that a carrier landing in a disabled aircraft was exceedingly dangerous, not just ot the airplane's pilot but to every man aboard.

There continued to be some concern in the naval technical community about the Skyraider's capacity to handle the impact of a heavy landing on a carrier deck. Despite progressive improvements throughout the AD-1, -2, -3 and -4 models aimed at strengthening the aircraft, the Skyraider was not as sturdy as it appeared when slammed down with brutal force on a pitching deck. The eventual 'fix' was the improvement in Navy carrier decks which occurred in the 1950s, but in the meanwhile Skyraiders limped home from Korean missions and 'catching the wire'— getting a clean pull with the tailhook—continued to be a difficult task.

Carrier War

Valley Forge was joined, as part of Task Force 77 in the Yellow Sea, by USS *Phillippine Sea* (CV-47) and USS *Leyte Gulf* (CV-42). Flying in mixed strike forces with F9F Panthers and F4U Corsairs, the seablue Skyraiders were tasked with eroding the enemy's means to wage war by chewing up vehicle

THESE PAGES AND OVERLEAF
When USS Essex *(CVA-9) embarked on a Korean combat cruise lasting from 16 June 1952 to 6 February 1953, Commander Stanley W Vejtasa's Air Group Two had two Skyraider squadrons aboard. VA-55, with an 'S' tailcode, had AD-4 aircraft bearing side nunmbers in the 500 series and was led by CDR L W Chick. VC-11 had an 'ND' tailcode. was equipped with AD-4W Skyraiders with 55 series side numbers, and was skippered by LCDR D W Knight. These six views of Skyraiders on that cruise were taken by participant Chuck Kaufman and made available through the generosity of Paul D Stevens.* Essex's *straight wooden deck was a challenge to the Skyraider pilots. So, too, were North Korea's MiGs and anti-aircraft guns* (Chuck Kaufman)

columns, supply points and rail lines. There was much improvising to be done with mission profiles, ordnance loads, and other abrupt realities: naval aviators quickly saw that their peacetime training had not been fully realistic.

In September 1950, the invasion of Inchon and the capture of much of North Korea by friendly forces made it seem that the conflict would soon end. It was a heady time, and ground troops kept pushing forward while Skyraiders appeared overhead, demonstrating their ordnance-carrying capability. This grew more formidable as the Skyraider itself was improved: an AD-4 aircraft typically set forth on a mission carrying ten 5-inch HVAR (high velocity aircraft rockets) and two 1000-lb (554-kg) bombs. These weapons could be rippled or delivered singly, the Skyraider pilot typically choosing the right moment to inflict the ordnance on enemy troops.

In November 1950, amid the worst Korean winter in many years, the Peoples Republic of China joined the fight, sending half a million troops virtually overnight to swarm down on the US Army 2nd

Infantry Division at Kunu-ri, the First Marine Division at the Chosin Reservoir, and other UN forces. In terrible cold, in dismal flying weather, Skyraiders were tested in the difficult task of close air support. Skyraider pilots, many of them new ensigns brought on active duty for the conflict, learned to drop bombs within a few feet of friendly troops.

Newsreels of the period, shown in cinema houses, depicted Skyraiders hurtling across snow-covered Korean slopes and laying napalm and other ordnance on top of the onrushing Chinese. News reporter John Elliott flew on a combat mission in a Skyraider and, describing the experience, seemed preoccupied with the weather. 'Inside the narrow metal seat below the pilot, the temperature was 15 degrees Farenheit. The skin of your arm, if it had sweat on it, could stick to metal.'

Before China's entry into the war, an opportunity had been missed to bomb the bridges across the Yalu River which provided a major supply line for the bad guys. Afterward, B-29 bombers and other aircraft including AD Skyraiders were permitted to attack the bridges. But their efforts were impeded by the toughness of the bridges themselves and by rules which prohibited 'pulling out' over Manchurian airspace on the far side of the Yalu. Several of the key bridges were still standing on 9 November 1950 when carrier-based naval aircraft mounted a major effort against them.

Skyraiders and Corsairs attacked the southern approaches to the rail and highway bridges at Sinuiju and the two highway bridges near Hyesanjin. A Navy F9F Panther pilot managed to shoot down a MiG-15 while this was going on, but the 1000-lb (554-kg) bombs carried by AD Skyraiders were insufficient to break the bridge spans. By December, it no longer mattered: the Yalu froze over and the enemy was able, not merely to drive vehicles across the river, but to run railroad tracks over the ice! One Skyraider pilot looked down at this, frustrated at being unable to attack because there was no *way* to attack without flying over China—and cursed.

Close-In Combat

In the very difficult conditions which prevailed in Korea, the AD-2 -3 and -4 Skyraiders first established their ability to fly and flight at breath-takingly low level. There were verified accounts of pilots returning to their carrier decks with pieces of

F4U Corsairs and AD Skyraiders from USS Boxer *(CV-21) rendezvous off the North Korean coast on 15 August 1951, apparently at the conclusion of a combat mission since no ordnance is visible. Corsairs belong to VF-791, Skyraiders to VA-702, both Naval Air Reserve squadrons called to active duty for the conflict (USN)*

ABOVE
Provided through the courtesy of naval authority Norman Polmar and probably taken by CAG Richard C Merrick, this look from a circling AD-4 Skyraider shows Mark 13 torpedoes exploding on the sluice gates of the Hwachon Dam in May 1951 (USN)

LEFT
Carlson's Canyon, they called it, when Skyraiders first went in low to attack bridges being used by the Chinese and North Koreans. By October 1951, when this Skyraider from USS Boxer (CV-21) attacked a bridge along a river near the Korean coast, bridge-busting had become almost routine for the Douglas-built warplane (USN)

trees embedded in their round R-3350 cowlings. One pilot killed a Chinese infantryman with his four-bladed, sixteen-foot propeller and returned safely to his ship. Though it had only the crudest bombsight, which would not lead-compute a target, the Skyraider proved far more accurate in delivering ordnance than the fast jets of newer origins.

On several occasions, carrier-based Skyraiders tangled inconclusively with North Korean propeller-driven aircraft. One strike destroyed a number of Ilyushin Il-10 aircraft on the ground. In the first year or two of the war, before the enemy established his night harassment capability, the air-to-air encounters produced no result.

The typical life of a Skyraider pilot aboard an aircraft carrier brought long hours of aggrevation, brief moments of terror, little sleep, and continual challenge.

For the AD Skyraider pilot embarked aboard ship, a typical mission began with an 0400 wake-up while the carrier was preparing to turn into the wind for launch. Pre-flight briefing was held in the ready room, where the skipper of the squadron or the division leader for the day would go over weather, target and Intel materials with his pilots and crews. (Many of the Skyraider models in combat in Korea, like the AD-4NL, had a second crewman positioned behind and below the pilot).

By this hour, the overall operations of the carrier air group had been coordinated among senior officers who were often the first up, last asleep. The ordinary Skyraider jock thus knew by perhaps 0530 where he was going and when. Last stop before the aircraft was the equipment deck, where the pilot checked out pistol, life vest, and his personal helmet. The plane captain responsible for a particular Skyraider—an assignment which never changed, although the *pilot* might not necessarily fly the aircraft with his name on it—would be waiting at the aircraft.

A typical mission with an 0700 launch might be an interdiction strike against a North Korean railhead some 200 miles (322 km) from the carrier. If it was a combined strike involving more than one aircraft type, the AD Skyraiders would launch first, while an HO3S-1 'plane guard' helicopter hovered near the ship's fantail ready to rescue the crew if trouble arose. Corsairs would follow and escorting jets, Panthers or Banshees, would be last to leave the carrier deck.

Varying cruise speeds would be adjusted so that the strike force would 'hit the beach' together, perhaps at 0730 hours, with fighter escort positioned to block any trouble. In point of fact, MiG-15s on the far side of the Yalu River were not often a direct threat to carrier aviators, having largely been isolated and contained in the region known as 'MiG Alley' by Air Force F-86 Sabres.

Though its flying weather was more forgiving than that of another Asian country where Americans would fight a generation later, Korea could be 'a real bitch,' as one flyer put it, in the winter and the interior of the AD Skyraider was somehow never warm enough. Even the 'winterized' versions, AD-4L and AD-4NL, were never warm enough.

Weather Factors

Depending on the time of year in a war which seemed at the time to be endless, the Skyraider driver was likely to be shivering or sweating by the time he arrived over target around 0815 hours.

The MiGs were not often present, but the flak could be treacherous. North Korea seemed to be littered with heavy-calibre guns which left ugly black smudges when their shells exploded at altitude. Attacks on a target were usually made in two-ship

sections, with timing and direction being varied to confuse the enemy gunners, but there can be no denying that communications faults sometimes led to confusion in the strike force, too.

The typical pilot, hopefully, rolls in at 0815, follows his section leader down across paddy fields wedged into a narrow canyon, and drops his bombs squarely on a railroad marshalling site being used for enemy supplies.

If he's hit, the Skyraider pilot knows that his aircraft can sustain tremendous damage and still get him safely back to the carrier. If he's hit bad, he still wants to try to make it to the coast and hope to mate up with an HO3S-1 chopper, but if it's winter he doesn't want to ditch: he'll survive in those ice-cold waters no longer than twenty minutes at most.

If he's unfazed, the Skyraider pilot recovers safely on the carrier around 1030 to 1100 hours and the cycle can be repeated for an afternoon mission. Once in awhile, if he's lucky, the Skyraider aviator will learn that he's getting the chance to go after a really juicy target—like a bridge or a dam.

Bridge Bombers

On 2 March 1951, a Corsair pilot from USS *Princeton* (CV-37) happened upon a bridge at Kilju where rail lines from Manchuria went across a deep canyon. It was a breathtaking sight, this bridge. The completed portion of the bridge ran about 600 feet (183 m) across the canyon, and stood at least 50 feet (15 m) off the canyon floor. Five concrete abutments supported six steel spans. Clearly, this was a spot where a few well-placed bombs would choke off a vital communist supply crossing.

Princeton's carrier air group 19 under CDR Richard C Merrick had a typical force structure for the period. Of its three fighter squadrons, VF-191 operated F9F-2B Panthers while VF-192 and VF-193 flew F4U-4 Corsairs. A detachment of squadron HU-1 was equipped with the Sikorsky HO3S-1 helicopter. The air group also had a composite squadron, VC-3, with AD-4N Skyraiders and a medium attack squadron, VA-195, with earlier AD-4 Skyraiders. It was the last-named squadron, under LCDR Harold G (Swede) Carlson, which went after the bridge on 3 March.

In 'Carlson's Canyon,' the Skyraiders went in low, delivered bombs with remarkable accuracy, and disabled one span while damaging the others. Night-fighting Corsairs and AD-4N Skyraiders appeared during the nocturnal hours to slow down North Korean efforts to repair the structure.

On 15 March 1951, Skyraiders went after the bridge again, using napalm this time. Swarming down in a splash of blue quickly punctuated with the red-yellow of explosions and fires, they incinerated the trusses used in repairing the structure. With a further strike on 2 April and some help by Air Force

AD-4 aircraft 122355, side number M-501, launches from USS Valley Forge *(CV-45) on a Korean combat mission with three box-finned, 2000-lb (907-kg) bombs on board. Hovering in the background is Sikorsky HO3S-1 'plane guard' helicopter, ready for action if the AD-4 pilot splashes into the drink* (USN)

B-26 Invader night intruders, the bridge across Carlson's Canyon was severed.

Many believe these very successful strikes led to James Michener's novel *The Bridges at Toko-ri*. The Skyraider was not to be immortalized in lore, however. In the novel, the strike aircraft were F2H-2 Banshees and in the film version Swede Carlson's job was done by William Holden in F9F-5 Panthers. There *was* another motion picture of the period. 'Men of the Fighting Lady', in which Skyraiders did appear—playing themselves.

Following the Chinese entry into the conflict, the Korean War settled into a series of operations without major changes in the front lines and with little clear picture of who was winning. Operation Strangle, launched on 31 May 1951, was designed to cut off the Chinese and North Korean troops on the battlefield by severing the supply lines to their rear. Vehicles, trains, bridges, rail lines, tunnels—anything that could be reached with a bomb qualified as a target. This air effort, in which AD Skyraiders, played a major role, inflicted serious harm to the enemy's war effort.

Drone Controller

In mid-1952, the US Navy began using the first guided weapons to be employed during the Korean conflict. An F6F-5K Hellcat pilotless drone with a single 2000-lb (992-kg) bomb aboard was 'guided' via remote control from an AD Skyraider mother aircraft. The pilot aboard the Skyraider simply engaged the target visually and drove the Hellcat drone into it. Six F6F-5K drones were launched on 28 August 1952 from USS *Boxer* and, guided by a Skyraider, were effective against a bridge at Hungnam. In general, however, the pilotless drone was not a very accurate or useful weapon.

The 'winterizing' effort which produced the AD-4L and AD-4NL models (previous chapter) made the Skyraider an optimum warplane for the Korean conflict. Fast jets were not yet accurate enough to take on a narrow bridge span or hostile troops in close contact with friendly ground forces, and the Navy and Marine Corps never really mastered this job with the Panther or Banshee. The Skyraider was far from perfect—its bombsight was crude even for the time and its 20-mm cannons were prone to malfunction—but the oft-mentioned endurance and load capacity of the Skyraider made it, truly, a flying dump truck.

Handling a big, ungainly propeller aircraft on the crowded and narrow carriers of the period—a British invention, the angled deck, had yet to be introduced—was no easy task. Visibility over the nose of the tail-dragger AD-4 was severely limited and a carrier deck offered little leeway to S-taxi, so a deckhand sometimes stood on the wing to guide a pilot when he manoeuvred aboard the ship. The old-style wooden decks were brutal on tyres and, although the Skyraider finally was properly stressed for hard landings, an unusually hard setdown could still wreak damage. On occasion, a Skyraider pilot found himself thrown over the side into the drink, and it was never an easy task to get out of the airplane—in the air, on deck, or in the ocean.

By August 1951, and to a considerable extent some months before than, the Korean War had become a stalemate. Vast armies faced each other across narrow stretches of ground with little real movement, forward or backward. Truce negotiations were begun, first at Kaesong and later at Panmunjom, but moved at a glacial pace. (As a footnote, the eventual ceasefire was signed only by field commanders—*not* governments—and in altered form, those negotiations continue to this day). Skyraiders continued to provide close support but they also ranged over the rear areas up to the Yalu River, continuing to strike bridges, convoys, marshalling yards.

According to an account which appeared at the time in *Naval Aviation News*, one Skyraider pilot actually *captured* a group of Chinese Communist soldiers! Like many tales from the period, this one is a bit nebulous (no carrier or unit are mentioned by name), but the story is that an AD Skyraider pilot with all of his ordnance expended noticed a platoon-sized unit of Chinese moving up a hill and began buzzing them. Though he could not shoot, they did not hesitate to fire upon him. So busy were the Chinese trying to get rid of the pesky Skyraider—like a man trying to swat a fly off his back—they failed to notice a group of US Marines who surrounded them. After only a brief surge of ground fighting, some two dozen Chinese soldiers surrendered, and were herded toward the American Marines by the still-present blue Skyraider!

Enter the MiG-15

The MiG-15 jet fighter entered the war with the Chinese. Thumbing their noses at the self-imposed political constraints which forbade US airmen from attacking China's airbases, Mao Tse-tung's air force kept numbers of MiGs basking in the sun on the north side of the Yalu, where they could have been bombed to oblivion if only the rules would have allowed.

It is easy to forget, but the MiG-15 was a stunning revelation to Western eyes, almost as much a shock as was Sputnik seven years later—proof that intelligence on Soviet capabilities was sparse and that Moscow's engineers could design a world-class fighting machine. So little was known about the MiG, in fact, that in some quarters it acquired an image of mystery and of invincibility.

An intrepid F4U Corsair pilot altered this vision somewhat by shooting down a MiG-15 in an air-to-air engagement. (Marine Capt Jesse Folmar, unfortunately, was lost in action shortly after this remarkable feat). No Skyraider ever matched this accomplishment, although Skyraiders did tangle with the MiG and must have made some communist fighter pilots exceedingly nervous.

Having proved themselves against a bridge, Skyraider pilots now confronted the mighty Hwachon Dam which loomed high above the Pukhan River. An attempt by Army rangers to immobilize the dam during a daring raid on 11 April 1951 was unsuccessful. By the end of April the dam had been briefly captured, given up to Chinese attackers, and bombed—again, with little measurable success—by

B-29 Superfortresses. 240 feet thick, with both faces reinforced by rocks, the dam simply wasn't going to give way to a free-fall bomb dropped from high overhead. By 30 April, a decision had been made to charge *Princeton* with attacking the great dam, using a weapon that no one had tried in combat for some years—the aerial torpedo.

The choice of ordnance should have been obvious, but it wasn't made immediately. A hard lesson had to be learned on 30 April 1951 as six Skyraiders lugging 2000-lb bombs and 11.75-inch Tiny Tim air-to-ground rockets made an assault on the dam while covered by five F4U-4 Corsairs. As could have been easily predicted (and probably was), the rockets simply bounced off the Hwachon Dam's sturdy structure. The bombs made no significant dent in the dam, either.

Torpedo Bomber

Torpedoes. VA-195 skipper Swede Carlson, who had done such a fine bridge-busting job just weeks earlier, discovered that most of the men in his squadron had never *seen* a torpedo.

It was apparently little more than happenstance that *Princeton* had twelve Mark 13 torpedoes on board. Ordnancemen knew little about how to move, arm, and load the cylindrical devices. Only three VA-195 pilots had ever actually dropped a torpedo from a Skyraider. Still, it was clear the effective delivery of the Mark 13s would make it possible to cripple the Hwachon Dam's floodgates and deplete all or part of the dam's swollen reservoir. If successful, such an attack would thoroughly disrupt the Chinese and North Korean forces in the area. It should be noted, however, that the floodgates were formidable, being 40 feet wide, 20 feet high, and 2½ feet thick.

The mission was mounted on 1 May 1951. *Princeton* sent eight torpedo-armed Skyraiders aloft, five from VA-195 and a trio from VC-35. Twelve F4U-4 Corsairs flew cover while a pair of F9F-5P Panthers from squadron VC-61 followed behind for post-strike reconnaissance. Although Carlson's name is closely associated with the mission (and his squadron, ever since, has been nicknamed the Dam Busters), the strike was actually led by *Princeton*'s CAG, CDR Richard Merrick.

Years after the fact, when some of the participants are gone and the ferocity of that dirty little Asian war is overshadowed by another Asian war which followed, it is a challenge to the mind to actually see, and feel, Carlson's crews assaulting the Hwachon Dam. The heavily-laden Skyraiders had to wean their way around 4000-foot mountain peaks to get into position for a run-in on the dam. The Skyraider pilots then had to roll in, align themselves on the dam's floodgates using the Skyraider's rather primitive sight, and, as one pilot put it, 'hope like hell their flak didn't get lucky while you were chasing

your shadow across the water and aiming at the dam'.

In fact, anti-aircraft fire—which had been intense earlier—proved relatively light. The accompanying F4U-4 Corsairs, whose job was to put enemy flak batteries out of commission, found themselves with little to do but orbit overhead and observe the attack. Six of the eight torpedoes actually dropped on the Hwachon Dam struck true and two of them smashed a floodgate, sending a deluge of water pouring down on the valley below.

As noted in a superb analysis by Barrett Tillman and Joseph G Handelman, DDS, Merrick, Carlson, Bob Bennett and the other Skyraider pilots did a first-class job on the dam. Scrutiny of the reconnaissance pictures brought back by the Panthers showed one floodgate destroyed and the bottom half of the other blown away. Release of water from behind the dam had holed the western abutment.

Other missions by other Skyraiders blew holes into, tore apart, transformed into confetti, or otherwise pulverized a variety of targets so numerous as to be encyclopedic. But there was something special about busting the dams. Few events, before or since, have been so symbolic of modern warfare. We have already mentioned the book and the motion picture *The Bridges at Toko-ri*—can anyone forget William Holden as the young naval aviator, meeting Grace Kelly in a steam-filled Japanese bath?—but apart from the glamour of this kind of combat, there was the certain knowledge of its effect upon the

Shook II is the nickname on this AD-4 Skyraider from USS Boxer (CV-21) carrying its bomb load toward bridges spanning the Changjin River on 25 April 1951. Photo was taken from an F2H-2 Banshee which cruised at about the same speed as the laden Skyraider (USN)

enemy. Said one pilot, 'You could see the results of your work.'

Marine Combat

It was a different and perhaps less glamorous war for the Marine Skyraider pilots who pressed the conflict from land bases and flew their Skyraiders right over the heads of fellow Marines while delivering ordnance to the Chinese and North Koreans. In spring and fall, a Marine base like the one at Pohang—its revetments and taxiways paved with pierced steel planking (PSP)—was remembered by everyone present for its mud, mud, mud. At Chinhae, conditions were so appalling that the crudely-built control tower, scarcely more than a box on stilts, was named 'Dogpatch Tower'—and bulldozers were used at times to clear the mud. The Skyraider, in fact, proved relatively forgiving in a muddy environment.

When they weren't wallowing in the mud on the ground, the Marines came screaming down out of the sky to move mud in the enemy's midst. 'The ideal

OPPOSITE
*Testing the kinds of
ordnance employed in
Korea, AD-2 Skyraider
122339 lifts off at
NATC Patuxent River,
Maryland* (USN)

LEFT
*Although taken at
Patuxent, Maryland,
this low-level view of
Skyraider 122339 is not
dissimilar to what North
Korean and Chinese
soldiers saw when the
aircraft was flying close
support* (USN)

environment for a pig,' commented one member of a
Marine squadron. This was a bit of an insult to the
porcine inhabitants of this planet for the truth was, no
pig sty anywhere from Pohang to Peoria could match
the enormous clouds of 'liquid crud' sent flying into
the air by the Skyraider's R-3350 engine when the
wet season hung over the base.

MSGT Doug Williams was a Marine 'wrench
monkey' at Pohang and used his mechanical talents
on Skyraiders, Corsairs and Tigercats. Now retired
in Reston, Virginia, he remembers the experience
with mixed feelings. The pilots, they loved that R-
3350 because it would pull them through the air with
enormous bursts of power. We mechanics hated it.
That doggoned engine was the most difficult to work
on that I ever encountered. And at times even a most
minor problem would make it necessary to strip the
whole damn thing apart and put it back together.

'This was bad enough working indoors on
spotlessly clean hangar floors or ship's decks. But in
the primitive conditions we had in Korea, putting a
Skyraider engine back together again was sheer hell.
At times, a fairly significant amount of our work had
to be performed *outdoors*. Also, we had a helluva
problem with our pipeline of parts. We would have
too many of one thing, not enough of another. There
was a particular kind of cotter pin we needed for the
metal cowling which was simply never available and
in the end we had to have them made by Koreans in
the village near the base. I was in Korea for fifteen
months and this condition never improved.'

An interesting sidelight to the Marine Corps
experience is that many pilots were non-
commissioned officers (NCOs) and warrant officers.
In the Korean War, Marine Skyraiders were still
flown by men as low in rank as staff sergeants. The
other services had long since dispensed with the
'sergeant pilot' who played such a vital role in World
War 2. Marine Skyraider squadrons such as VMA-
331 probably had far more experience, including
combat experience, in their ranks than did compa-
rable Navy squadrons.

The Marines also operated the AD-4W Skyraider
early-warning aircraft with its 'guppy' radar shape
beneath the fuselage. Colonel R D (Red) Edwards
was a very junior pilot with squadron VMC-1,
serving at Pohang and Kimpo airbases. 'The guys
who should rate the most mention were the radar
operators who squeezed into the back of our AD-
4W,' says Edwards. 'Those young troops were gung-
ho and they were willing to undergo a lot of sacrifice
to enable us to go aloft, day or night, and peer over the
front lines toward the bad guys. Thanks to our
radarmen, we were a kind of primitive spy plane,
keeping watch for the bad guys and vectoring our own
aircraft toward them when necessary.

'Even though the AD-4W was heavier and more
difficult to fly than the AD-4 I'd trained on in the
United States, I always loved flying that model. And
of course even on the AD-4W model, the pilot had
pretty good visibility except to the rear. Sometimes I
had the feeling, though, that I was nothing more than

a glorified chauffeur, doing the driving job so that the guy in the back seat could do the work.

'We had this one radar guy, I swear to you, he wore a green visor over his forehead and squinted into his scope. He was the kind of guy who would be called a nerd today—skinny, bespectacled—but could this young Marine *ever* operate that radar! Our primary job was to watch for enemy aircraft and they did not come down all that often, but this kid had them on the scope instantly whenever they showed up and he never lost them, no matter what they did.' As will be seen, the job of watching for Chinese and North Korean aircraft may have been without its glories but it was a mission that had to be performed.

Biplane Combat

Although no Skyraider pilot succeeded in downing a MiG in Korea, the Russian-built Polikarpov Po-2 biplane proved a different kind of adversary for the Douglas attack aircraft.

North Korea, although it never seriously challenged US control of the air in any other way, sent Po-2s with fragmentation bombs to harass American bases at night. These 'Bedcheck Charlie' missions were reported in the Press as nuisance raids, designed to hamper the sleep of American GIs, but they had military significance: a 17 June 1951 nocturnal attack on Suwon airfield by two Po-2s which came in a shrieking torrent of noise destroyed one F-86 Sabre, damaged eight others, and wounded several Americans.

The Po-2, was brought into the world by Nikolai N Polikarpov, a gifted engineer of the Stalin era who died in 1944. Little-known outside the Soviet Union, the biplane may actually have been built in greater numbers than any other aircraft type in history. It was a spartan flying machine, reflecting the drabness of the workers' society which produced it—largely fabric-covered, pulled through the air by a two-blade wooden prop driven by a 115-hp M-11K engine and just barely capable of the impressive speed of 100 (161 km/h) mph in level flight. Incredibly, the nocturnal Po-2 consistently eluded a variety of American warplanes which pursued it, although one was shot down by a Douglas B-26 Invader, another by a Grumman F7F-3N Tigercat.

As the war continued, Bedcheck Charlie's visits to US airbases occurred intermittently, with Corsairs and F3D-2 Skyknights joining the aircraft types which scored Po-2 kills. Other Soviet propeller-driven types, including Lavochkin La-11s and Yakovlev Yak-18s joined in the night harassment missions. US Marine Corps Corsair pilot Lt Guy Bordelon shot down five of these night hecklers in June and July 1953 to become the only propeller-pilot air ace of the war.

The Skyraider's turn came on 15 June 1953 when no fewer than nine after-dark raiders assaulted Seoul.

An AD-4NL Skyraider from Marine composite squadron VMC-1, with Major George Linnemeier as pilot and CWO Vernon Kramer as radar operator, was vectored to intercept a Po-2 when friendly ground fire interrupted the chase.

Linnemeier was again vectored into the area and Kramer picked up the Po-2 on his radar scope. Apparently flying very low over night-lit Seoul and the Han River, Linnemeier found the intruder and poured 20-mm cannon fire at it. The North Korean aircraft went into a steep left bank and exploded against the ground.

The nocturnal raids were inexpensive from the enemy's viewpoint and possibly would have continued no matter how effective the measures taken against them. Few threats were more of a challenge to naval and Marine aviators, who—once again—had never received any training for this sort of thing. The Skyraider did not lose its forgiving nature when darkness arrived, but air-to-air combat at night continued to be 'something else,' and not every man was up to it.

The evening after the Linnemeier kill, Major Robert Mitchell and CWO William Lundy, also from VMC-1, were aloft in the Seoul/Inchon area when their efforts to intercept a night intruder were repeatedly upset by communications failures which caused friendly gun batteries to open up on their AD-4N Skyraider. Major Mitchell closed on three separate night hecklers and damaged one with 20-mm fire, but interference by friendly ground fire prevented him from scoring a kill and nearly made him a casualty.

Skyraider pilots made additional efforts to 'nail' the troublesome nighttime raiders. But although the AD Skyraider was probably highly suitable for operations against Bedcheck Charlie, no further kills were scored. This sidelight of the Korean War continued through to the end of the conflict, with the Americans never finding a fully satisfactory remedy for the Po-2.

The 27 July 1953 armistice ended the unpleasant Korean episode in American history (although, as will be seen, not hostile acts in the region or action by Skyraiders). The people who keep numbers tell us that thirteen aircraft carriers participated in the Korean War (all, at one time or another, carrying Skyraiders). 167,552 sorties were flown by US Navy carrier-based aircraft and another 107,300 by the Marines. 120,000 tons of bombs were dropped. Carrier-based pilots, according to the number experts, destroyed 37,000 enemy buildings, 6400 rail cars and locomotives, and 4500 trucks. They reportedly killed a milllion Chinese and North Korean troops.

With the signing of the armistice, Navy and Marine air units began to rotate home. The AD Skyraider remained in the area, however. Ed Heinemann's remarkable Douglas aircraft would be 'in business' in the Far East for a long time to come.

Chapter 4
AD-4
The Skyraider with the Kangaroo Roundel

In the grand scheme of things over the fifty years since the Skyraider's conception in the Statler Hotel, the aeroplane's service with the United Kingdom was but a brief sidelight.

Never try, however, to dismiss the aircraft when talking to the Britons who maintained, worked on, and flew the Douglas AD-4W Skyraider AEW.1—to whom the anglicized Skyraider was a very special machine indeed. To quote the Royal Navy's Vice-Admiral J D Treacher, ex-skipper of Nos 778 and 849 Sqns, 'This large rugged aircraft epitomized all the best characteristics of American carrier aircraft with good forward vision for the pilot, a tough under-carriage and responsive controls. Its arrival in the Royal Navy not only introduced the large airborne radar but such novelties as the first bone-domes, electrically powered cockpit canopies and pilot's seats; electronics which happily continued to function and even thrived on life in the deck park.'

The Skyraider AEW.1 did, in fact, serve the Royal Navy for ten years and, as Admiral Treacher points out, 'There can be few aircrew who failed to recognize the sterling qualities of this aircraft or to remember her with affection.' (The quote, with permission, is from an excellent monograph by the British Aviation Research Group which is, alas, out of print).

The 'spy in the sky' function described by the term AEW (airborne early warning) dates, in manner of speaking, to the Battle of Fleurus in 1874 when France's Colonel J-M J Coutelle employed a balloon to snoop out intelligence on the arraying of his enemy's forces. During the First World War, 'scout' aircraft and balloons gave new refinement to efforts to reconnoiter an enemy's activities. The subsequent addition of radar to this aerial snooping role culminated in the AEW aeroplane and its mission.

In American parlance, aircraft which perform this role were once called 'radar picket planes' and their function has more recently been subsumed by the term AWACS (airborne warning and control system), a term used in some quarters as a synonym for today's US Navy Grumman E-2C Hawkeye carrier-based aircraft. Far more precise, however, is the British term AEW which, simply, refers to the use of radar and other electronic sensors to warn the Fleet of an enemy's approach.

Radar itself is, of course, a British invention dating to 1936 but the first sets were far too large and unwieldy to be carried aloft by aircraft. No radar-equipped picket planes were available during the 1945 invasion of Okinawa when low-flying Japanese *kamikaze* (divine wind) suicide aircraft swarmed down on US warships and inflicted terrible damage.

In 1945, however, the US Navy began work on Project Cadillac, the first serious attempt to develop a Fleet AEW capability, placing AN/APS-20 radar aboard a Boeing PB-1W (B-17G) Flying Fortress and, during the same period, a carrier-based Grumman TBM-3W Avenger. According to one source, as many as 35 AEW-equipped Avengers were actually available for use before VJ Day but did not see action. The Avenger was, in any event, the first shipboard AEW aircraft and by 1948 was supplanted by the AD-3W Skyraider, the version which preceded the AD-4W delivered to the Royal Navy.

Flying Radar

A brief history of the Fleet Air Arm's Skyraider AEW.1 (and the disposition of some of these aircraft in Sweden) has already appeared in this narrative. The AD-4W Skyraider AEW.1 carried a crew of three—pilot and two observers located side-by-side below and behind the cockpit. The AN/APS-20A radar installation, an improvement over the AD-3W kit and a rather remarkable advance in technology for its day, weighed no less than 1000 lb (454 kg) and was

ABOVE
At the French airbase at Chateaudun in the late 1970s, AD-4 Skyraider 126877 has finally come home following years of service in sub-Saharan Africa. Many of the French AD-4s are now becoming available for use as civilian 'warbirds' (Chris Pocock)

TOP
Seen at El Segundo on 16 January 1951, the date of its first flight, aircraft 124761 was the 52nd AD-4W 'radar picket plane'. From June 1951 to March 1952, it served the US Navy with VC-12, making four carrier deployments. The aircraft was delivered to Britain on 16 January 1953 and acquired the Royal Navy serial WT761. Its service career ended on Boxing Day, 1958, when it was broken up for spares (courtesy Hal Andrews)

AD-4NA Skyraider 126921 of training unit ATU-301 at Cabiness Field near Corpus Christi, Texas in 1957. Though its 3T tailcode, 170 side number and green/white cowl trim stand out sharply, the paint scheme on the aircraft is severely weathered. Red/white training paint scheme in background replaced blue and remains in use today (Doug Francis)

TOP
A little forlorn, Marine Corps AD-4B Skyraider 132261 sits in the grass at the Corps' museum, Quantico, Virginia, on 3 June 1978. This Skyraider is a candidate for restoration (Robert F Dorr)

ABOVE
At low level over the Philippine Sea in 1959, AD-6 Skyraider 135367 of the 'Arabs' of VA-115 carries out a sortie from USS Shangri-La *(CVA-38). The grey/white paint scheme adopted by the Fleet in the mid-1950s was used for the remainder of the Skyraider's service life* (Doug Francis)

TOP
*Douglas UA-1E (former AD-5U) 132463, side number
AF-412, once operated by the Oceana, Virginia-based
'Tigers' of VA-65 aboard USS* Enterprise *(CVAN-65) is
seen at Andrews AFB, Maryland on 19 November 1983
awaiting turnover to a museum for restoration (Joseph G
Handelman, DDS)*

ABOVE
*The former AD-5, now redesignated A-1E, finally joined
the Air Force in the mid-1960s and went to war in
Vietnam. This A-1E belongs to the USAF's First Air
Commando Squadron at Bien Hoa in 1964 (USAF, via
Mike Byers)*

OPPOSITE
*Comparative views, taken in 1966 at Bien Hoa AB, South
Vietnam, show US Air Force A-1E Skyraider before and
after addition of Southeast Asia-style camouflage. Aircraft
carrying standard Mark 82 500-lb (227-kg) bombs wears
the grey/white paint scheme Air Force inherited from
Navy; aircraft carrying napalm tanks wears the T.O.
1-1-4 camouflage which became standard (Perrin Gower)*

THIS PAGE
*A-1E Skyraiders of the US Air Force's 602nd Air
Commando Squadron at Qqui Nhon, South Vietnam in
about 1966. Skipper of the Qui Nhon detachment, Major
Dafford (Jump) Myers was rescued at A Shau by First
Air Commando Squadron's Major Bernard Fisher (Perrin
Gower)*

TOP LEFT
A-1G Skyraider (former AD-5Q) 139598 (TC) of the
First Special Operations Squadron (former First Air
Commando) at Nakhon Phanom, Thailand in 1969. Note
different canopy structure as compared with A-1E in
previous photo. Mark 82 500-lb (227-kg) bombs with
'daisy cutter' extender fuses were considered a good 'people-
killing' item of ordnance (James Doolittle 3rd)

LEFT
A-1E Skyraider 132410 of the Qui Nhon Detachment,
602nd Air Commando Squadron, in flight over Southeast
Asia in 1966 (Hubert G King)

ABOVE
Though it suffered battle damage on several occasions,
A-1H Skyraider 139622 of the South Vietnamese Air
Force (VNAF) looked in excellent condition when long-
time historian Dave Menard snapped this view at Da
Nang prior to February 1966 (David W Menard)

ABOVE
Seen at Stockholm's Bromma Airport on 13 June 1974,
SE-EBL, a target-tug operated by the company Svensk
Tjangst AB, *is actually an AD-4W Skyraider 127922*
which earlier served with the Royal Navy. First flown in
August 1952, 127922 once had Royal Navy serial WT987
while serving with No 849 Sqn. It also briefly wore civil
registry G-31-3 (Lar-Erik Lundin)

ABOVE

Four-ship formation of Royal Navy Skyraider AEW.1s. These aircraft are WT103 (124085) as '323/CU'; WV179 (124115) as '324/CU'; WT964 (124112) as '325' and WT121 (124121) as '326'. D Flight of No 849 Sqn operated these aircraft in the same blue paint employed by the US Navy. The 'CU' tailcodes on the first two Skyraiders indicates their base was at Culdross in Cornwall (courtesy R J Mills, Jr)

TOP

AD-4W Skyraider 126867 was refurbished and was, in effect, 'like new' when it was delivered to the Royal Navy and became WV181, coded 414/J. The aircraft is seen here, its powerful R-3350 engine turning over, in the UK in 1957 (Victor Flintham)

Aircraft 124083, in this previously unpublished view, was not one of the AD-4W Skyraiders which went to Britain but was identical to them. White trim on vertical stabilizer is typical of squadron VC-11 aboard USS Boxer *(CVA-21). This launch from the carrier deck took place on 30 August 1955* (Courtesy Peter B Mersky)

RIGHT
Aboard USS Lake Champlain *(CVA-39) with the Sixth Fleet in the Mediterranean in this unpublished 28 December 1955 view, AD-4B aircraft 132364 of Marine squadron VMA-324 taxies forward. This 'nifty fifties' Skyraider was similar to, but not identical to, the several AD-4 sub-variants delivered to France for use in the war in Algeria* (Courtesy Peter B Mersky)

reported to have cost one million dollars per set when new. Also employed aboard such aircraft as the Lockheed P2V Neptune and Grumman AF-2W Guardian (the 'hunter' part of an anti-submarine 'hunter-killer' team), the AN/ASP-20A radar set had an output of 1 megawatt (one million watts), fed to an 8-foot (2.44-m) elliptical dish aerial rotating inside a bulbous fibreglass radome which, itself, was the source of considerable structural problems and, under some circumstances, severe vibration, hindering the success of the AEW mission.

This radar set operated in what was then called S-band (today's E/F band). Shorter wavelengths were not possible because of the time taken (even at the speed of light) for each pulse of energy to reach the target and return. For example, at a target range of 100 miles (161 km), the time base could not run faster than 1000 per second or the pulses would not return before the next one went out. Thus, the PRF (pulse recurrence frequency) could not be higher than 1000.

LEFT
It took considerably more than the eight men shown here to keep a Royal Navy Skyraider flying. These men are either attaching or removing an underwing drop tank. Visible at wing leading edge are the 'Suez stripes' worn by aircraft during the 1956 intervention in Egypt (via Glyn Owen)

ABOVE
Less known as a photographer than as an emerging writer on the aviation scene, Roy Braybrook snapped this view of '415' at Culdrose some time after 30 October 1958, the day it acquired the three-digit call number. Aircraft WT121 (bureau number 124121), a typical AD-4W Skyraider AEW.1, served with US Navy squadron VC-11 before reaching the Royal Navy (Roy Braybrook)

In the early stages there were also severe problems with the massive reflections from the ground or sea, which tended to obliterate important targets such as enemy warships or low-flying aircraft. Most of these early difficulties were resolved, in the early days, by the sheer artistry of the unsung radar operators aboard the AEW Skyraider who compensated for the inadequacies of their system with a kind of personal magic. The AN/APS-20A was, of course, substantially improved over time and was later used aboard the Fairey Gannet AEW.3 and the Avro Shackleton, among other aircraft types. Eventually, this radar was able to detect the bad guys out to a distance of about 150 miles (240 km)—not yet very impressive, but certainly of some utility.

While the exact sequence of delivery of these 'radar picket planes' to the Royal Navy is a somewhat convoluted tale, it is instructive to remember them as having been turned over in four separate groups of 19, 11, 4 and 16 airframes.

The first two groups, totalling 30 Skyraiders, were ex-US Navy aircraft. The original batch of 19 went from the El Segundo plant of the manufacturer to NAS Norfolk, Virginia for installation of electronics

TOP LEFT
In 1956, AD-4W Skyraider AEW.1 aeroplanes WT952, WT957, WT960 and WT961 fly in close formation. In foreground is WT961 (bureau number 127959) which had made its first flight on 21 February 1953 and reached the UK a month later. This aircraft remained in service until December 1958 (via Glyn Owen)

BOTTOM LEFT
In this view, the fuselage number 421 is worn by aircraft WT958, alias bureau number 127956. On 13 April 1957, this machine overran the runway at Culdrose during a maintenance test hop and ploughed through the perimeter fence, being damaged so badly that it never flew again (via Glyn Owen)

THIS PAGE: TOP
Skyraider WT965 of D Flight, No 849 Sqn, is launched from HMS Albion in 1956. Bureau number 124124 had operated with US Navy squadron VC-12 before joining the Royal Navy. This Skyraider finished its flying career in 1958 and was reduced to spares in 1961 (via Glyn Owen)

MIDDLE
Another view of the Royal Navy's WT761, wings folded, wheels chocked, not far from the control tower at Culdrose. Britain chose to retain the US Navy's basic aircraft colour—glossy sea blue—just as it had done in an earlier era with American-made Hellcats and Wildcats (via Glyn Owen)

BOTTOM
Royal Navy Skyraider WV179 (bureau number 124115) was another machine which served with the US Navy's squadron VC-12 before reaching Her Majesty's Service. On 20 November 1959, this aircraft ditched in Caglian Bay while returning to HMS Victorious (via Glyn Owen)

before their US service and, afterward, were refurbished at NAS Quonset Point, Rhode Island before being shipped to their British receipients via Norfolk (again) and Glasgow. The second batch of eleven followed a similar route although some of these were modernized at NAS Alameda.

With the exception of bureau number 125772 which had been operated by Air Development Squadron One (VX-1), all of these veterans had served with Composite Squadrons Eleven and Twelve (VC-11, VC-12).

The Royal Navy's third group, four Skyraiders, was 'diverted' from US requirements and delivered to Britain without any previous US service. The fourth group, 16 Skyraiders, was a 'new build' batch which began their service careers in British livery.

'Radar picket planes,' as the US Navy called them, were aboard some carriers during the 1950–53 Korean conflict but were never actually tested against enemy ships and aircraft. The reluctance of enemy forces to attack aircraft carriers in Korea, Vietnam and elsewhere, in fact, seems to have lulled us into a complacency which is worth a separate volume in itself and which was intact at least until the 1982 Falklands fighting. This was not, however, the last time the AEW Skyraider served in a combat zone. Though it is frequently forgotten by those of us on the colonial side of the Atlantic who provided neither participation or support, British and French forces went to war in Suez in 1956.

The sea gloss blue Skyraider with black and yellow 'Suez stripes' (similar to the Normandy 'invasion stripes' of World War 2) was an impressive sight, even if its use in the Suez action may have been a violation of the Mutual Defense Assistance Pact (MDAP) terms under which the aircraft was supplied to the Crown. During the Suez campaign, hard-pressed British soldiers were delighted to learn that with some internal re-arrangement the Skyraider

could bring more than 1000 cans of beer to troops on the beaches.

Suez Recalled

The purpose of the Suez operation, it may be remembered, was to secure the vital canal belonging to Egypt—and involved extensive cooperation between Israel, France and the UK.

Richard Anderson, a retired US Navy engineer, remembers the way the Skyraider was used by British pilots during Suez. 'Here was one of those situations which are so typical of war,' Anderson recalls. 'A large number of missions were compacted into a very narrow time frame, meaning that long-established maintenance and repair schedules had to be scrapped. The Skyraiders had to be flown around the clock, and shortcuts had to be found to keep them in the air. It quickly became apparent that, despite the difficulties of coping with the R-3350 engine, the AEW Skyraider was really much stronger and capable of withstanding greater punishment than anyone had believed.'

In point of fact, few details have survived about Skyraider flying during the Suez affair. Anderson: 'It isn't really clear whether they ever had any bogies [hostile aircraft] to vector fighters against.' The image of a Skyraider with invasion stripes landing on the beach to bring beer to the troops is an evocative one, but not too illustrative of the missions flown. An official history notes that during the Suez operation, also called Operation Musketeer, C Flight of No 849 Sqn, Royal Navy—then headed by Lieutenant Commander D A Fuller—operated its Skyraiders from HMS *Albion* to provide early-warning protection and ship-to-shore communication. It appears that pilot and radar operator spent long hours, day and night, flying around in circles and looking in vain for the bad guys.

It is worth mentioning that the British Skyraiders were flown all over the world in an era when Britain was still viewed as a global naval power. Thus, one AD-4W belonging to No 849 Sqn acquired a kangaroo marking planted squarely in the middle of its dignified British roundel, during a stopover in Australia. A typical cruise began on 6 January 1956 when D Flight of the squadron went aboard HMS *Albion* for an extended tour of the Far East. The expedition lasted more than three months and before returning to home base at Culdrose in Cornwall, the Skyraiders had flown on exercises with the India and Pakistan navies.

It was the coming of the Fairey Gannet which marked the end for the Royal Navy's Skyraider after nearly a decade of service. The bulky, turboprop-powered Gannet AEW.3 had been designed for the AEW role and arrived on the scene early in 1960. Thereafter the Skyraiders were, in effect, obsolete.

Wearing the 'invasion stripes' associated with the Suez operation of 1956, aircraft WV178 (bureau number 124111) lifts off from HMS Albion during the Anglo-French intervention (via Glyn Owen)

LEFT
The French Air Force's AD-4N Skyraider 126969, wearing an MK code, towards the end of its fighting days in 1973. France's Skyraiders served throughout Africa and participated in several brushfire conflicts (via Norman Taylor)

ABOVE
A 'straight' AD-4 Skyraider flies tail behind an AD-4W early-warning aircraft of squadron VC-11 as both pass over a pair of Essex-class carriers during flight operations in the 1950s. The bureau number of the latter is not visible in the photo, but the AD-4W could easily be one of the US Navy machines which were eventually transferred to the Royal Navy (USN via Peter B Mersky)

Madagascar Interlude

In 1965–67, it was this author's lot to serve a tour of duty in Tananarive, Madagascar—then a quiet backwater (more recently a *revolutionary* backwater with its capital renamed Antananarivo) left in rather dreary shape by the French colonists who granted its independence in 1960. In those days, we used to say that if the British had been there, as in Kenya, they'd have left behind the infrastructure to support a newly emerging nation; if the French had been there, they'd have taken everything of value out. But in the mid-1960s, the French had not yet taken out their paratroops at Ivato Airport or their AD-4 Skyraiders.

The Great Red Island, Madagascar is called, because of the red laterite deposits which lie exposed on the hills and in the land, as if some surgeon had forgotten to close a wound. You simply have not seen a Skyraider until you've seen an unpainted, silver AD-4 taxying in a cloud of red dust, its R-3350 wheezing and belching, oil dripping back into the swirling red flecks. The American air attache in Tananarive in those days, Colonel Robert Reiminsnider, had flown B-17s in World War 2. He would sit at Ivato, watch the silver French Skyraiders taxi by, and observe, 'It looks and sounds like Double-U Double-U Two all over again.'

We never really knew what sort of mission the French were flying in Tananarive in those days. The silvery Skyraiders would leap aloft from Ivato, swing out towards the Indian Ocean some 100 miles (161 km) to the east, vanish for a couple of hours, and return. No hostile threat existed out in that direction or, for that matter, anywhere else. When a carrier on-board-delivery (COD) aircraft from USS *Enterprise* (CVAN-65) called at Ivato in 1965—while the carrier was en route to combat operations in Vietnam—the COD received a Skyraider escort.

France's acquisition of the proven Douglas product resulted from *l'Armee de l'Air*'s need to replace the weathered P-47D Thunderbolts being used in the conflict against *Font de Liberation Nationale* (FLN) forces in Algeria.

The end of the line, almost. The Royal Navy's WT949, alias AD-4W Skyraider 127947, seen at Stockholm's Bromma Airport in June 1970. Civil registered as SE-EBB, the aircraft was operated by Svensk Flygjanst AB as a target tug. In 1986, two of these Swedish-registered machines were returned to the UK to be rebuilt as 'warbirds' (Lars Soldeus)

No fewer than 113 former US Navy AD-4 Skyraiders were supplied to France and served eventually with squadrons EAA20, 21 and 22 (*Escadre Aerienne de l'Attack*). The airbase at Chateaudun, primarily a ferrying stopover in virtually the geographic centre of France, is understood to have become the logistics and servicing facility for the Skyraiders, although all served overseas in such African backwaters as Somalia, Chad, the Central African Republic, Gabon, Upper Volta, Madagascar.

Ed Collins, an American diplomat, was in Gabon in 1971–73 and had observations similar to the author's. 'At that time [rather late in the history of French Skyraider operations], the airplanes were supposedly being flown by native Gabonese pilots. The truth was, they couldn't handle it and we had this bunch of [French] pilots who were like something out of the old Flying Tiger movies. They would walk up to the bar in flight suit, hitch their boot up on a rail, and begin drinking and telling flying stories. One day, I saw one of them stand at the bar 'flying' with his hands, telling tall tales. A few minutes later, he walked out to the airplane, kicked the tyres, and hopped in. I'm not a hundred per cent certain he violated the rule against drinking and driving, but it sure looked like [he did].'

Colonel Claude Rosello, France's air attaché in London, never flew anything smaller than a Boeing C-135F, but he remembers a French friend who made the rounds of steamy, backwater African capitals serving tours of duty in the erstwhile AD Skyraider. 'I never heard that the plane or the R-3350 engine were easy to maintain,' says Rosello. 'In fact, there was a conscious effort made to use only the most experienced mechanics on the Skyraider. I can tell you, however, that some of our pilots regarded the airplane as the best "fun flying" they ever experienced.' Apparently, duty in a remote hellhole had its compensations and one of them was more real flying, less paperwork.

Very little is known about the AD-4 Skyraider aeroplanes which France resold to Cambodia in the early 1960s, although one US official remembers seeing a pile of Skyraider-related wreckage at Phnom Penh Airport some ten years after the delivery. It is thought that the AD-4s were used by Khmer fliers only briefly and only during one of the intervals when Cambodia's peripathetic Norodom Sihanouk was in power and pursuing a 'neutral' position. It is possible the AD-4s were involved in the 1964 shootdown of a USAF Cessna O-1 Bird Dog, on a mission in South Vietnam, which strayed inadvertently into Khmer territory.

Too, the final disposition of Cambodia's AD-4 Skyraiders remains unknown. There does not appear to be any truth to a report that some of these aircraft were returned to US control and ended up at the Military Aircraft Storage and Disposition Center at Davis-Monthan AFB, Arizona.

Swedish Skyraider

The Swedish Air Board's reached its decision in 1961 to acquire a dozen of the Royal Navy's AD-4W Skyraider AEW.1 aircraft. Neutral as she might be, albeit with few of her guns pointed in a westerly direction, Sweden has traditionally maintained stronger armed forces than the NATO nations of Scandanavia, and a real need was seen for a dedicated target-tug aeroplane. Scottish Aviation Limited at Prestwick received the contract to convert the AD-4Ws to target tugs, deleting all of the equipment that went along with the AEW mission (including 'guppy' radome) and installing a winch operator's station in the crew position heretofore occupied by a radar operator.

The twelve Skyraiders were painted a brilliant yellow and acquired Swedish civil registry (SE-EBA through -EBM with -EBJ missing). They operated from Stockholm's Bromma Airport, the small municipal field which noise-conscious local residents have been trying to close for years. *Svensk Flygtjanst Aktiebolaget* (Swedair Limited) flew the aircraft and provided pilots and maintenance people under contract to the Swedish Air Force.

One machine, SE-EBH (ex-WT959, bureau number 127957) was destroyed by fire while taxying at Lulea in northern Sweden on 8 September 1968 after half a decade of target-tug service. This was replaced by the 13th Swedish Skyraider, aircraft WT849 (bureau no 126849) which was delivered to Stockholm without being converted, went through the conversion to target-tug at Bullofta, and became SE-EBN. This machine, too, was lost when it landed with the undercarriage up at Midlanda Airport, Sundsvall, on 6 May 1971 and was consumed by fire. The newspaper *Sundsvalls Tidning* headlined the event with a single word, '*Slutet*', which means literally, 'It's finished'.

Little has been written about the target-tug work performed by these aircraft, but there can be no doubt that flying the Skyraider in Sweden was at times a difficult task. Apart from the Skyraider fires noted above, aircraft SE-EBH (before its subsequent demise) lost major sections of its left wingtip in an air-to-ground collision with a radio mast!

Long Story

The full story of foreign Skyraiders (not including those in Vietnamese service, to be discussed in chapters 8, 9) would fill a volume in itself and is somewhat outside the scope of this 'Air Combat' series. Suffice to say that wherever the Skyraider went, air arms found it to be an exceedingly effective warplane. Even after it was in widespread service with other users, the Skyraider was in fact only beginning its service and combat life.

Chapter 5
AD-5
The 'Wide Body' in the Viper's Pit

In 1948, a study for the US Navy's Bureau of Aeronautics (BuAer) concluded that an improved Wright turbo-compound engine should be used to power a new Skyraider, to be designated AD-5. The proposed new engine was vital to plans for several aircraft types then on the drawing board, but the powerplant—as it turned out—was too heavy and too large for practical installation, even on an aircraft as large and sturdy as the Skyraider.

By the beginning of fiscal year 1950 (1 July 1949)—perhaps the bleakest period in naval aviation as far as the availability of purchasing dollars was concerned—the new Wright engine was officially determined to be impractical. At the same time, hard-pinched for funds in a false era of peace (Americans as yet unaware that the Russians had exploded their first atomic bomb), the US Navy was cancelling a number of aircraft contracts. With a stroke of the pen, BuAer reduced one order for 185 AD-4W and AD-4N airplanes to 53. This was the era when admirals in the Pentagon were being told to write on both sides of a piece of paper and reduce the number of carbon copies in order to save money. In this austere budget climate, the first known use of the AD-5 designation died a little-noticed death.

'Second' AD-5

The AD-5 designation was resurrected just as the second half of this century began. The familiar-looking Skyraider coming from the Douglas production line was not to look distinctly unfamiliar, its 'new look' marked by a widened body and a completely rearranged canopy configuration, to say nothing of the airplane's internal fit.

At one juncture, Rear Admiral Stanley Laurance was called up on the hill (to use the Pentagon insiders' term for Capitol Hill, where Congress meets) to justify a relatively minor appropriation for BuAer which included support for the AD-5 programme. 'I might as well have been thrown into a pit of vipers,' remembers Laurance, who is not a naval aviator but made several flights in the Skyraider. It was an era when *any* request for military funding was subject to rigorous scrutiny. 'To my surprise, nobody asked a question about the aircraft and everything went fine.'

The second AD-5 proposal, made while spending constraints crimped planning efforts in those final months before the Korean conflict, was for a Skyraider which would combine the anti-submarine warfare (ASW) 'hunter' (S for Search suffix) and 'killer' (E, signifying attack, suffix) into one airframe, so that instead of developing AD-5E and AD-5S, a single Skyraider would be able to both detect and attack Russian submarines. The point bears repeating that in the late 1940s and early 1950s, the fast-growing size of the Soviet Union's undersea force was a 'hot' issue in the Pentagon and among the Navy staff.

Not quite as scalding, however, as the Korean War. The onset of conflict on that peninsula forced

TOP RIGHT
The Navy's sea gloss blue colour scheme appears almost black in this 17 November 1952 view of AD-5 Skyraider 132478 in 'clean' condition on the ground at El Segundo. In order to increase crew size, the 'wide body' AD-5 introduced a lengthened fuselage and enlarged tail. Over time, numerous missions were carried out by this bigger and heavier version of the Skyraider (via Hal Andrews)

RIGHT
Often referred to as an AD-5W, the first aircraft in the 'dash-five' series (124006) was, in fact, a converted AD-4 and lacked the 'guppy' radar installation associated with the -5W early-warning aircraft. 124006 is seen on an early test flight over California (Douglas)

The Marines used all manner of Skyraider, witness this 1955 view near El Toro, California of (from bottom) AD-5W, AD-5, and AD-4W (via R J Mills, Jr)

TOP RIGHT
A trio of 'wide-body' AD-5 Skyraiders of VMFA-331, with aircraft 132648 in trail, fly over Miami on 26 July 1955 (via Paul D Stevens)

the admirals to set aside their 'combined AD-5E/AD-5S' notion. In due course, the idea was resurrected, but with the decision that the new configuration would be employed for an AD-5W airborne early warning aircraft—capable of detecting both aircraft *and submarines* threatening the Fleet but not really equipped to attack either.

This first change in Skyraider configuration noteworthy enough to leap out and catch the onlooker's attention finally became reality on 17 August 1951 with the first flight of the side-by-side seating AD-5 variant. The first machine in the series is usually listed as an AD-5W and was probably the only 'dash five' to have been converted from an earlier AD-4 aircraft, bureau number 124006. In fact, it lacked the radar and electronics suite planned for the -5W and was employed for proof-of-concept flight tests.

Pilots liked the design though they found it a bit more sluggish to handle than its predecessors. They also noticed immediately that, in this radical departure from previous Skyraiders, you did not 'roll in' to the right. On the left (or port) side of the aircraft, the pilot simply did not have visibility to succeed in a calculated manoeuvre which required peeling to the right.

The Skyraider had never been an easy plane to get out of, and the AD-5 was no easier to escape in an emergency. When the Navy issued document AN 01-40ALE-1 dated 15 March 1964, the Flight Manual for the AD-5, it was especially thoughtful towards the right-hand passenger who might have to leap from the airplane. No one ever reads such things at the right time, of course, and it is always difficult to bring them to mind when needed in the rush of a crisis, but the manual—mindful that more than one naval

TOP LEFT
The most dramatic change ever made in American aircraft markings was the Navy's decision to shift from blue to gull grey (on top) and white (on bottom). These AD-5W Skyraiders of squadron VAW-12 wear the new paint scheme over the Mediterranean (USN)

LEFT
Introduced in February 1955, the US Navy's new paint scheme called for gull grey on top and glossy white undersides. It was a dramatic change from the former sea gloss blue which had adorned carrier-based aircraft. The new paint scheme is demonstrated here by AD-5W Skyraiders 135163 and 135183 (AJ-720 and AJ-702) of squadron VAW-12, winging over the Atlantic near USS Forrestal *(CVA-59) on 29 August 1960 (USN via Peter B Mersky)*

ABOVE
Sitting in sunshine on the ramp at NAS Corpus Christi, Texas on 15 April 1958 is an AD-5Q Skyraider with the nickname 'Night Hawks' painted beneath side number 842 on the cowling. This version had a rear cockpit design slightly different from other 'wide-body' Skyraiders (USN via Peter B Mersky)

TOP LEFT
AD-5W Skyraider 139599, with distinctive under-fuselage 'guppy' bulge, has tailhook extended and mainwheels partly down as it apparently makes a 'go-around' from an angled-deck carrier in the middle to late 1950s (USN via Peter B Mersky)

ABOVE
Deck crew in foreground run for cover as this AD-5 comes in too fast, catches the first wire off-centre, and pitches forwards. 'No-grade' will almost certainly be the verdict on this messy arrival (USN)

In the 1950s, a tailcode consisting of a number followed by a letter almost always meant a training unit, the 3T on this AD-5 Skyraider signifying ATU-301 at NAS Corpus Christi, Texas. Pilots got some 'dual' time in 'wide-body' aeroplanes at times, although most training was conducted in single-seaters, the instruction being absorbed prior to first solo. Aircraft 132487, wearing standard red/white trainer paint scheme in this superb view unearthed by researcher Peter B Mersky, gives a remarkably clean appearance sitting on the Corpus ramp on 28 April 1959 (USN via Peter B Mersky)

aviator had slammed against the high vertical fin of a Skyraider on the way out, warned:

'. . . care must be taken to keep the body as low to the [canopy] rail as possible during bailout. Upon gaining the proper position for bailout, give a vigorous coordinated push with the feet and pull-push with the hands and arms while diving for the wing . . .'

It was enough to make a pilot want to ditch under any circumstances! What right-seater could possibly be expected to act properly while the airplane was on fire and tumbling to earth? 'The body should be doubled-up with the legs and arms well tucked-in upon leaving the airplane. Bailout should be accomplished from a point as far forward as possible. This will provide the individual with some protection from the slipstream during the initial roll over the [canopy] rail and will aid in clearing the horizontal stabilizer'. Talking to the person *sitting on the right*, the manual continued, 'Whenever possible, bailout should be made from the right side of the airplane. . .'

A contortionist with a delayed-release parachute, a strong resistance to the effects of gravity, and plenty of luck would have been able to hit the silk from an AD-5 without fear or hesitation. A normal-sized naval aviator was almost certain to express a preference, whether academically or in an actual emergency, for bellying the aeroplane in.

Fortunately, few people ever had to parachute from a 'wide-body' Skyraider until a generation later and by then—to get well ahead of the story—an extraction system was developed.

Fits and Starts

Development of the AD-5 had been cancelled at the outset of Korean fighting, then reinstated while Americans searched for Korea on their maps, and finally continued at a markedly reduced pace. Although the first flight occurred while more than two years of war lay ahead, the AD-5 was never employed in Korean combat.

The AD-5 Skyraider *was* genuinely distinctive in appearance and evoked nicknames ranging from 'wide-body' to 'fat face'. It certainly demonstrated, both literally and figuratively, the 'stretching' potential of the basic Skyraider design. Its after-section, where additional crew members were housed beneath a plexiglass cover often tinted a deep blue, became known forever as the 'Blue Room'—not merely for the colour, but for its implication of elegance, size, and spaciousness.

AD-5Q early-warning Skyraider 132521 flying over Atlantic seas during a sortie from NAS Quonset Point, Rhode Island on 6 September 1982. The aircraft belongs to squadron VAW-33 (USN)

ABOVE
Mishap on a carrier. EA-1E Skyraider 139562, coded GDP835 and belonging to squadron VAW-33, is twisted around at the wrong angle following a not fully successful 'trap' of the arresting hook wire aboard USS Lake Champlain (CVS-39) on 19 September 1964 (USN via Peter B Mersky)

ABOVE RIGHT
In about 1968, A-1E Skyraider 135202 of the 1st Special Operations Squadron at Pleiku wings over Vietnam in standard Southeast Asia T.O. 1-1-4 camouflage. Barely visible on the nose of this 'Spad' is a Kangaroo emblem, suggesting that someone connected with the aircraft may be Australian (USAF)

RIGHT
The city of Saigon is the backdrop in war's 'early days', circa mid-1964 as A-1E Skyraider 132469 of the 1st Air Commando Squadron passes over the South Vietnam capital. At this beginning stage of the conflict, Skyraider is still painted in the grey/white scheme it wore with US Navy (USAF)

The side-by-side configuration offered additional crew space both beside the pilot and behind him for an AD-5W airborne early-warning sub-variant which the US Navy wanted as a replacement for the AD-4W and in which the Royal Navy also exhibited interest. There was considerably more space than was ever fully utilized for any of the regular missions to which the Skyraider was assigned, and aircrews always had plenty of room to carry extras on long trips. No one knew it yet, but the widened aircraft was a candidate for many chequered and varied missions ranging from counter-insurgency (a term introduced into the jargon a decade later) to ambulance duty. The early-warning mission drove the design and dictated the configuration.

'New Look' AD-5

To bring about revision of the fuselage and achieve an

Another variation of the photo on page 96 shows EA-1E (ex-AD-5W) Skyraider 139562 of squadron VAW-33 making a not very successful landing aboard USS Lake Champlain (CVS-39) on 19 September 1964. Champlain and other ancient carriers of the era had wooden decks, which were not kind to Skyraider tyres (USN via Peter B Mersky)

TOP RIGHT
133888 veers left on a flight on 1 June 1961 (USN)

increase in cockpit area, the Skyraider was lengthened by 23 inches (112 cm) and the crew space, accommodation, canopy and windshield were all redesigned. This brought about a minor shift in the aeroplane's CG (centre of gravity), making it necessary to move the improved R-3350-26W engine (specified for 2800 hp but in due course rated at just under 2700) eight inches forward. A visibly increased

vertical tail had almost 50 per cent more surface area (although the Skyraider was to remain an aircraft not amenable to those with clumsy feet on the rudder pedals). Other changes in the AD-5 configuration included an airscoop at the leading edge of the vertical fin, re-arranged radio equipment and antennas, and deletion of the side-fuselage dive brakes.

The Marine Corps was very interested in the side-by-side Skyraider and believed that, apart from those specialized versions which eventually were built (217 AD-4W airborne early warning craft; 138 AD-5N night-attack aeroplanes; 54 AD-5Q electronic countermeasures machines, and a single AD-5S submarine-hunter), the new configuration would also be highly suitable for a 'straight' AD-5 attack plane.

As a straightforward air-to-ground strike aircraft, the AD-5 had wing pylons which were enlarged and raked forward and provisions were made for a new and sturdy centreline pylon. The AD-5 looked as if it could carry a heavier bomb load than previous Skyraiders and, in fact, it could: one typical load which could be taken over a fairly long range was a centreline box-finned 1000-lb (454-kg) bomb of World War 2 vintage, two huge 11.75-in Tiny Tim air-to-ground rockets on those large, forward-swept inboard pylons (called 'stubs') and no fewer than twelve 5-in HVAR (high velocity aircraft rockets) on outboard wing stations. The AD-5 also retained armament of four wing-mounted 20-mm cannons.

'Dash Five' Performance

The AD-5 was credited with a combat range of no less than 1044 nautical miles. Its ability to travel long distances and/or loiter for long periods over a target was duly noted by the Marines in the 1950s and would eventually become important to the Air Force in a war that lay ahead. Dimensions included a wing span of precisely 50 ft and fuselage length of some 40

EA-1F Skyraider 133581, side number VR-779, comes in for recovery aboard USS Constellation *(CVA-64) in the Gulf of Tonkin on 14 September 1967. The 'electric Skyraider' helped to protect the Fleet during the Vietnam conflict and was the last version of the aircraft to serve aboard carriers in the battle zone* (USN)

RIGHT

In September 1958, Detachment 45 of squadron VAW-12 serving aboard USS Essex *(CV-9) was commanded by LCDR William S D'Epagnier. This September 1958 view of the squadron's AD-5Ws over the Pacific survives replete with the names of all crew members: aircraft 132765 (side number AP-701) crewed by LTJG E A Cooper, LTJG R D Sundbye, and AN M D Timothy; 135191 (AP-704) by LTHG J E Shay and AD3 D L Cyr; 132743 (AP-702) by LTJG S L Zwick, LTJG C P Mooney and AT2 G E Rojan. Note that the two aircraft in foreground have the canopy shape associated with this variant while third Skyraider, for reasons unknown, does not* (USN via Harold Andrews)

ft 1 in (as compared with 38 ft 4 in for the AD-1, -2, and -3; 38 ft 10 in for the AD-4, -6 and -7). The AD-5 was 15 ft 8 in in height, three inches taller than the AD-1, -2 and -3 but the same height as the other variants.

Maximum speed of the enlarged AD-5 was 344 mph (553 km/h) at 10,000 ft (3048 m). The aircraft had a service ceiling of 26,000 ft (7924 m), although crews did not like to fly the Skyraider on oxygen and high-altitude missions were seldom a realistic part of Fleet operations. Combat range is listed in one manufacturer's document as 1344 miles (2150 km). Range or combat radius, in fact, varied considerably according to the amount of external fuel carried and the size of the ordnance load, but pilots who flew the AD-5 were always impressed with its 'long legs' and its loiter capability.

What's remarkable about the AD-5 is not that it existed in several variants but that it did not exist in more. The Marines in particular saw the sturdy, wide-bodied aircraft as a kind of ace-in-the-hole which would take care of a wide range of missions, giving the Corps a multi-role capability at minimal cost.

Apparently without participation by BuAer's AD-5 'class desk officer', whose recommendations weighed heavily in purchasing decisions, Marine officers discussed using the AD-5 to insert small teams of commandos and saboteurs (the term 'special operations' was not widely used then) behind enemy lines. Rather like the Westland Lysander of World War 2, the multi-place Skyraider would set down during the nocturnal hours at rough and unpaved strips to deliver black-garbed, black-faced men bent on secret tasks.

Marine Machine

More than a decade ahead of time, Marine planners were contemplating what later was called a counter-insurgency, or COIN, aircraft. It was reasoned that the Skyraider could carry enormous amounts of personal weaponry for a small team of ground combatants under the wing pylons in lieu of air-to-ground ordnance. A feasibility study was made of reducing the nighttime exhaust glow from the Skyraider to render it less visible to the enemy. This had caused concern during the Korean War, anyway, but no really practical remedy ever presented itself.

At the ready at NAS Quonset Point, Rhode Island on 8 February 1956, this AD-5W number 133773, side number NE-16, looks unusually clean except for the requisite exhaust deposits behind the cowling. This VC-12 airplane does not have the standard AD-5W canopy shape but is otherwise typical of the -5Ws which guarded the Atlantic Fleet for years (USN)

The novelist J E M Guinot, author of the acclaimed 'Americans at War' series, has written of hush-hush tests carried out with a Skyraider to evaluate its potential for inserting Marine fighters. His fictional account takes place at Fort Rucker, Alabama (a more likely spot for Army, rather than Marine, tests) and portrays both Skyraider pilots and Marine elite fighters as a rowdy band of mavericks. At one point in the fictional version, an intrepid pilot takes off under fire with one Marine lying atop the wing and clinging desperately to the leading edge. The characters are not unlike US Air Force people who belatedly flew Skyraiders a decade later, but the tests probably never took place. In preparing this volume, it was not possible to find out whether any actual COIN tests of the Skyraider went beyond the planning stages, but in one form or another the idea recurred throughout the 1950s and early 1960s.

At numerous times in its career, the AD-5—and occasionally other Skyraider variants—was evaluated as an aerial spray aircraft. To this day, consideration is being given to using surplus aeroplanes for aerial crop-spraying and firefighting duties, although the Skyraider is rather expensive to operate for this purpose. In the early 1960s, US Navy pilot Captain Doug Francis and others briefly tested a Skyraider rigged with spray bars for the purpose of delivering Agent Orange, the potent chemical used for defoiliation in Vietnam. This job was later performed by the Fairchild C-123 Provider, since the higher performance of the Skyraider was less important than the Provider's load-carrying capacity.

Many of the missions performed by the AD-5 never warranted a separate designation, nor received much recognition—artillery spotter, trainer, drone controller, 'hack'. There are also reports that the wide-bodied Skyraider may have introduced one or more members of the distaff gender to the 'Mile High Club', giving proof of an admiral's remark that, 'There's almost nothing you can't do in a Skyraider.'

As has been noted, another obvious role for the AD-5 Skyraider was that of hospital aircraft. Provisions existed for rapidly converting the combat AD-5 to this role, but it was rarely done—if ever—and the 'flying hospital' Skyraider never acquired a separate designation.

Personal Scrapbook

Walter Edison, a descendant of inventor Thomas Edison, was an Annapolis graduate (class of '49) and young lieutenant aboard USS *Midway* (CVA-41) in 1957 when tasked to head up a detachment of 'wide-body' AD-5W Skyraiders. 'I went into the assignment knowing that the Douglas design people, and Ed Heinemann in particular, had the reputation of building the best airplanes in the Navy,' Edison remembers, though others might award this accolade to Grumman. The young aviator's detachment of

VAW-12 (AK tailcode) brought together an unusual trio of creative names: one of Edison's wingmen was William Dean Howells, grandson of the famous poet, while another was William Shakespeare, not related to anybody.

'We flew early-warning missions throughout the cruise, even when the carrier was comfortably off the coast of New Jersey where nobody was likely to attack us. We paid more attention to what we were doing when we got to the western Mediterranean where the Soviets were just beginning to establish a naval presence.

'The AD-5W handled quite a bit differently from other Skyraiders. With that gigantic guppy hanging underneath, it was bulkier and less manoeuvrable and it had a nasty tendency to stall out. We also pushed the R-3350 engine to its limits for longer periods of time and you could see the results everywhere, including the messy oilspills aft of the cowl.'

Edison remembers that a Skyraider squadron—or a detachment of one, at least—was a place where men could take seriously both service to their country and the ever-present dangers of shipboard operations, without missing the chance to have some fun. While flying aircraft 135219, Edison was given the task of functioning as a COD (carrier on-board delivery), bringing some dignitary to the vessel from Naples. (The COD job is another of the Skyraider's unsung missions). Edison filled every empty cranny in the airplane with fresh Italian oranges and passed them out among his shipmates.

'There is nobody who deserves more credit for AD-5W operations than the enlisted radar technicians who flew with us all the time. I tell you, those guys were *dedicated*. It takes dedication to sit in a throbbing, orbiting airplane with your nose pressed up against a scope for hours at a time. Ironically, one of the best "scope dopes" I ever had was a guy who was also gripped by this unfortunate tendency to get airsick. Once in awhile, he had some cleaning up to do after a trap [carrier landing].'

The pilot of the early-warning AD-5W at times found himself in the most humiliating of worlds—chauffeur for crew members who had more responsibilities than he did, officer at the whim of enlisted men. In point of fact, it was the pilot who played a key role in alerting the Fleet when a threat was being tracked—AD-5W airplanes routinely engaged ships and aircraft of all kinds, often not knowing who they belonged to, other times knowing they were Soviet—but the feeling of being little more than a taxi driver was one that was hard to get rid of. 'There was plenty of room in the airplane and there was a tendency to sort of let the Skyraider fly itself and sit out the whole mission until something started to happen.'

*AD-5W Skyraider 132735 of squadron VC-12 at NAS
Quonset Point, Rhode Island, wearing side number NE-46,
in flight on 16 October 1956* (USN)

Lopsided Landing

Edison's detachment experienced only one mishap during his cruise. 'We had an ensign who could not get his landing gear down. This was a problem not at all characteristic of the Skyraider and I forget the reason, but he just couldn't get the mainwheels to extend fully. He finally got one down and locked but the other was hanging at an angle. He spent about two hours circling the ship trying to "fix" the problem and nothing happened. Finally, it was decided to attempt a landing.

'The LSO [landing signal officer] talked him in and he caught the number two wire very nicely. The AD-5W came slamming down on the ship's deck—supported by one wheel and that enormous guppy protrusion beneath the belly. Frankly, we had thought that all of that sensitive radar gear hanging under the airplane was going to come flying apart and, in fact, everybody had taken cover. The guppy radome *did* delaminate, but the whole thing stayed together and the AD-5W came to a stop just as nicely as you please, with no fire and no casualties.' The aircraft was repaired and returned to service.

Sea Duty

Not every Skyraider cruise was completed without fatalities and not every squadron enjoyed the dedication and conviviality of Edison's, but the life of an 'Able Dog' pilot in the 1950s was a fairly adventurous proposition. Aircraft carriers called on a variety of exotic and exciting ports, from Barcelona to Hong Kong. When not flying, attending to shipboard duties, or 'manning the rail' (standing dress formation), the Skyraider pilot could hoard his meagre salary ($375 monthly for an ensign in 1955) for the moments when the ship was in port.

Plenty of AD fliers were mature, married types whose idea of a good time was go to sightseeing, or take a ride in a rickshaw. Some brought their wives to Europe to join them, their squadron, and their ship. (There is never much revelry aboard US Navy vessels which, by tradition, are always 'dry,' i.e. no alcohol is permitted). A few indulged such passions as art exhibits and cultural museums, or at least a few claimed to.

But for those so inclined, especially the younger and unattached, every port of call meant new opportunities to cut up, carry on, get into trouble, and run the risk of incurring the displeasure of The Old Man—the CAG, or Commander, Air Group, who was all-seeing, all-knowing. Skyraider pilots seemed to have an uncommon ability to get into trouble whenever their ship brought them within range of new bars, new girls, new intrigue. A few hours in Catania (Sicily) or Pusan (Korea) offered fun, frolic and fleshpots to any man who wanted to partake—and compensated for long hours at sea and for separation.

Oddly enough, and this seems to be different from other realms of naval aviation, the men in competing Skyraider squadrons rarely seemed to get into fights with each other. It cannot be said that no bar-room brawl was ever initiated by an AD driver, but when it happened, the provocation was often a 'Heavy Puke' (a member of a heavy attack squadron flying A3D-2 Skywarriors) or, worst of all, one of the VF guys (a member of a fighter squadron flying F3H Demons or F11F Tigers). It must be emphasized that those occasions when Skyraider drivers conducted themselves as other than Officers and Gentlemen were unusual and atypical.

The AD Skyraider, for reasons never fully clear, produced a very tight community of naval aviators who looked out for each other throughout their careers. It was almost a clique. Flying this airplane created a special bond among them, and the bond remained even in later years when flying duties were left behind. Even today, long after the last Skyraider has left the Fleet, one can still walk into a certain admiral's office in the Pentagon, note the blue AD-5 model on his desk, and become an intimate friend merely by 'talking flying' with the assurance of one who has been there.

In the US Navy, however, there is almost no one left today who even *remembers* blue airplanes.

New Colours

While the Marine Corps adjusted to the 'straight' AD-5 in its ground attack squadrons and the Navy hunted submarines and enemy aircraft with subvariants of the same Skyraider, the post-Korean War US Navy moved dramatically to change the appearance of its aircraft. Since the early days of World War 2, most American naval aircraft had been painted a dark blue colour known officially as overall glossy sea blue (Federal Standard FS-595a colour 15042). Distinctive markings such as tail unit identifiers, or tailcodes, stood out in white letters. Occasionally a fin cap flash or other individual squadron colour might appear in a bright hue, such as glossy international orange trim.

After several years of studying camouflage schemes, including an exhaustive review of wartime experience with camouflage, the Navy and Marine Corps arrived at the conclusion that blue would no longer do.

New Paint Scheme

Everything changed forever with advance letter Aer-AE-421 sent to all naval commands on 16 February 1955, followed by a new painting document, MIL-C-18263(Aer) which went to the Navy and Marine Corps on 23 February 1955. The former document cancelled a Navy project to evaluate unpainted

AD-5Q Skyraider 132596 at NAS El Centro, California in July 1957 (USN via Harold Andrews)

combat aircraft—never relevant to the Skyraider, though many Banshees and Panthers had flown in natural metal—while the painting instruction enunciated the basic change: henceforth, carrier-based combat aircraft of the US Navy and Marine Corps were to be gray on top, white underneath.

Specifically, all except the undersides of carrier-based aircraft were to be painted in a non-specular light gull grey (FS-595a colour 36440, subsequently re-named light grey on 1 July 1971), while the undersides of the aircraft were to be glossy insignia white (FS-595a colour 178975). Henceforth, it

seemed, naval aircraft were to be camouflaged by using the open expanses of sky and sea as background. The new scheme looked very peculiar indeed on an AU-1 Corsair, for example, but in the AD-5 Skyraider community people quickly got used to it. Later in this narrative will appear the single-seat AD-7 variant, which was the first Skyraider to be delivered from the factory in the gull grey/white scheme.

Cold War Battle

Another event of the post-Korea mid-1950s must be mentioned in this narrative, involving not the wide-

body AD-5 but rather a formation of aircraft from USS *Philippine Sea* (CVA-47) which included AD-4W early warning craft of VC-11 and AD-5N night-fighter Skyraiders of VF-54. On 23 July 1954, a Cathay Pacific Airways Douglas DC-4 flying to Hong Kong was shot down by Chinese aircraft off the coast of Hainan, that vast island not far from the Vietnamese coast. Ten people, including three Americans, died.

On 25 July 1954, *Philippine Sea* sent a flight of two Corsairs, two AD-4Ws and two AD-4Ns prowling the coastal area southeast of Hainan. AD-4N pilot LCDR Paul Wahlstrom led the formation into a 180-degree turn just as two unknown aircraft appeared. An instant later, two Soviet-built Lavochkin La-7 prop-driven fighters came hurtling down, firing.

A wild melée ensued in which five of the six US Navy aircraft exchanged gunfire with the Lavochkin fighters, both of which were blasted out of the sky. (In this peacetime air-to-air engagement, one of the aerial kills was shared by two Skyraider pilots, the other by no fewer than five of the six American

participants). This incident was but one of a half-dozen or so peacetime air battles which took place in the Far East in the years immediately after the Korean War. A Skyraider would not have a chance to shoot down a hostile aircraft for more than a decade—and then, ironically, in almost the same location.

Tanker Skyraider

Throughout the 1950s and into the 1960s, Skyraiders laboured on with the Fleet. The advantages of the wide-body AD-5 continued to make themselves apparent. In 1956, the Navy suggested that the AD-5 be converted into an air-refuelling tanker. It took an exhaustive study by Douglas engineers to show that conversion to the tanker role would entail massive fuel volume and weight distribution problems. It was an interesting proposal—the North American AJ-2 Savage tankers then in use were becoming long in the teeth—but a Skyraider tanker with internal fuel was simply not an idea whose time had come.

of this refuelling capability—but the 'buddy' store has remained a part of the naval aviation scene until the present time. Douglas quickly fitted the D-204 store to the A4D-2 Skyhawk and in later years it was also employed by the Vought A-7 Corsair and other types.

MAD Gear

A lone AD-5 was tested in 1953 by air development squadron VX-1 at Key West, Florida, for the much-discussed submarine search-and-kill mission. Designated AD-5S and equipped with magnetic anomaly detection (MAD) gear, the AD-5S met Navy hopes in every respect, but the -S version was not put into production.

The 'wide-body' Skyraider in its many variants—now, of course, being seen through the Fleet in grey and white—remained in production until April 1956 when the 670th and last AD-5 was turned over to the Navy. The 'straight' attack AD-5, which the Marine Corps used successfully, eventually left operational service but the AD-5Q countermeasures variant was only beginning to make its own contribution.

Originally envisioned solely as a countermeasures aircraft, the AD-5Q was the beneficiary of yet another ambitious development programme at Douglas' El Segundo plant, this time aimed at producing a Skyraider capable of performing a dozen different functions. The project is confusing to look back at, following the passage of so many years, because it confuses the function of the AD-5N, -5Q, -5S and -5W suffixes in identifying specialized missions for sub-variants in the AD-5 series. Douglas's 'twelve airplanes in one' programme was aimed towards the goal of achieving nothing less than making the AD-5Q sub-variant, all by itself, capable of a dozen missions!

A Douglas-built utility kit enabled field modification of the AD-5Q so that, in a short span of time, it could become a basic day attack airplane, a night attack craft, target-tow or the anti-submarine hunter *and* killer. Other roles to which the AD-5Q could now be converted included the troop-carrying transport role. Relatively inexperienced plane captains and maintenance men were able to accomplish the conversion with a minimum of accessories and tools. One simply bolted on the appropriate package and the mission of the aircraft changed. The first conversion kit was turned over to the overhaul and repair division at NAS Alameda, California in 1956.

Another Skyraider paint scheme which appeared in the mid-1950s (actually authorized as early as 1953 but not seen on Skyraiders until several years later) was the red-and-white scheme adopted by training units.

With this scheme, a number of AD-5s as well as other versions shed their sea gloss blue for a sharply-contrasting flourescent red orange (Federal Standard

EA-1F Skyraiders of squadron VAW-33 over USS Forrestal *(CVA-59) in December 1964* (USN)

Instead, Douglas engineers came up with a separate idea which was remarkably innovative at the time and has remained with us to this day. Instead of rebuilding the AD-5, Douglas' engineers developed an external fuel storage package—referred to somewhat misleadingly as a 'buddy store' in later days—that could be used to refuel other aircraft in flight. The buddy store package contained a 300 US gallon fuel tank, a ram air turbine (RAT) employed to drive a hydraulic pump, a hydraulically-driven hose reel, and a 50-ft refuelling hose with a drogue.

Thus was born what eventually became the Douglas D-204 refuelling store, not merely the vehicle for a new Skyraider role but, in addition, an additional product for the company. As things turned out in the long run, Skyraiders did not often make use

FS-595a colour 11136) which stood out against glossy insignia white (FS-595a colour 17875). Pilot training squadron ATU-301 at Cabiness Field near Corpus Christi, Texas, where thousands of Skyraider pilots learned their trade, adopted the red-white colours in about late 1956.

Doug Franics, the pilot who'd tested the AD-5 with Agent Orange (unknowingly) was at Cabiness Field in 1957, a time of transition when Skyraiders were blue, grey/white and red/white. To make the scene even more colourful, the training base had every variant of Skyraider going back to the AD-2, the -1 being the only model to have been retired by then. 'It was a real sight to witness a gagle of ADs winging through the Texas skies,' Francis remembers. Certainly, it was a contrast to the colourless US Navy aircraft of today. 'Those Skyraiders made a kind of flying kaleidoscope.' Needless to say, one requirement for a trainer aircraft—high visibility—was met.

At Cabiness Field, Navy instructors took pilots who had flown only docile trainers, the North American SNJ Texan and T-28B Trojan, and introduced them to the Skyraider with a considerable amount of care and attention. As has been noted, the training syllabus did not include any dual-control flying in the Skyraider: when ready, the student was put into a single-seater and sent on his way. 'We had almost no accidents', remembers Francis, 'which is all the more remarkable because we had several landing strips in the Corpus Christi region and there were planes criss-crossing everywhere.'

When Francis joined the 'Arabs' of VA-115 for an Atlantic cruise aboard USS *Shangri-la* (CVA-38), it was different. Carrier operations always take their toll. In three months, the carrier lost three Skyraiders and two pilots.

Skyraider pilots, like others, were called upon to be firemen in 1959 when an electrical 'short' in an ammo locker aboard USS *Kearsarge* (CVA-33) set the ship ablaze and sent ammo rounds shooting all over the place. This, too, was the kind of mishap which, sadly, occurs often enough to be a regular part of naval aviation. Ed Collings, a seaman who spent two hours hunkering deep inside the carrier as the metal around him grew hotter and hotter, survived the ordeal to be told by a shipmate that several aeroplanes, AD Skyraiders included, had been chucked over the side. In the late 1950s, the US was at peace but uniformed service always entailed hardship and sacrifice.

This EA-1E Skyraider 135378 was employed for many years by the Naval Aerospace Medical Institute (NAMI) at NAS Pensacola, Florida. Shortly after this 26 February 1969 view, the aircraft was turned over to the US Air Force and almost certainly was used at Hurlburt Field, not far from Pensacola, to train men going to Vietnam to fly the type. Aircraft in background are (left) a Douglas C-117D and a Convair C-131F; above, a T-2 Buckeye shoots approaches (USN via Harold Andrews)

Chapter 6
AD-6
The Skyraider From the Horse's Mouth

Beginning in 1952 with an order for 325 airframes, the US Navy started to acquire the AD-6 version of the Skyraider, which came off production lines concurrently with the 'wide-body' AD-5. Essentially an improved version of the AD-4B, and optimized for the carriage of nuclear weapons, the AD-6 incorporated a jettisonable canopy, a hydraulic tailhook, and simplified electronic gear for ease of maintenance. The Korean War was still on and the AD-6 (which never actually fought in the conflict) enjoyed a high priority, but naval aviators were also convinced that the Skyraider would have a limited future once the war was over.

They were wrong.

Powered by the R-3350-26WD variant of the familiar 2600-hp engine—by now as famous for dripping oil as for supplying an enormous surge of power to the aircraft—the AD-6, in fact, proved to be remarkably long-lived. The AD-6 was also the first Skyraider to be built without a host of sub-variants bearing letter suffixes for specialized missions.

Considered by many the quintessential Skyraider, the AD-6 (which became the A-1H when US aircraft designations were changed on 18 September 1962) was in one sense the final model of the airplane since only a scant 72 examples of the AD-7 (A-1J) version appeared subsequently. First flown in June 1953, the AD-6 began its life while the Korean fighting was going on and became, in September 1960, the first US warplane to be supplied in quantity to South Vietnam. In between, Douglas delivered its 3000th Skyraider to the Navy in March 1956 and the final

A cross between the grey/white operational paint scheme and the red/white scheme adopted by training units, AD-6 Skyraider 139795 belonged to ATU-301 at NAS Corpus Christi, Texas and was seen minus its earlier 3T tailcode at Chicago's O'Hare Field on 17 December 1960 (Paul D Stevens)

AD-6 in August, 1956. The AD-6 was the most numerous Skyraider variant, some 713 coming off the Douglas lines.

AD-6 Milestones

An AD-6 piloted by CDR George Goodwin, skipper of the 'Blackbirds' of VA-45, became the first aircraft to land on the newly completed USS *Saratoga*, also in August 1956. Another interesting AD-6 milestone was passed in January 1962 when 'Knight Riders' VA-52 aircraft, AD-6s, operated from USS *Ticonderoga* (CVA-14) near Cape Horn—the first time any carrier-based aircraft had flown routinely in a region infamous for foul weather and raging seas during the South American summer.

Yet another AD-6 achievement was racked up when this version of the Skyraider went in September 1960 to a US Navy squadron being organized from scratch, the 'Boomers' of VA-165, at NAS Moffett Field, California, a unit which had not previously existed in any form.

The 'dash six' also introduced increased armour for the pilot. The need for improved armour was noted at various times in the Skyraider's life, partly through the efforts of LT Henry (Hank) Suerstedt who waged a one-man effort to persuade Douglas and the Navy that better pilot protection was essential.

The attention paid by Suerstedt and a few others to armour protection was the result of a disproportionately high number of casualities and aircraft losses in Korea caused by small-calibre gunfire. There was, however, some thinking to the effect that a heavy burden of armour was not such a good idea. A few pilots felt that the loss in airspeed imposed by any heavy armour package would be more harmful to them than being less protected.

TOP LEFT
Adopted in about 1956, the red/white paint scheme was intended to make training aircraft highly visible. AD-4NA Skyraider 125711 was wearing the scheme at NAS Miramar, California in 1957 (Merle Olmsted)

ABOVE
What appears to be a routine view of A-1H (former AD-6) Skyraiders unleashing ordnance is actually a part of a weapons demonstration for the Shah of Iran which took place off the US west coast on 2 May 1964 (USN)

LEFT
A nice ground view of the US Navy's innovative grey/white paint scheme. This view was taken after the change in aircraft designations and shows A-1H (formerly AD-6) Skyraider 135263 of the 'Valions' of VA-15, side number AB-512, at Richmond, Virginia on 14 March 1964 (Frank Hartmann)

In Korea, the US had captured several Soviet-built North Korean aircraft, including a Yakovlev Yak-9 fighter and an Ilyushin Il-10 attack aircraft, the latter a direct descendent of the Il-2 *Sturmovik* of World War 2. The Il-10 was taken to Cornell Aeronautical Laboratory in Ithaca, New York where engineers and technicians disected it to learn its inner secrets. It was rebuilt and flown for a time in US markings. Of particular interest was the heavy pilot armour of the Il-10, despite its origin in a society reputed not to place high value on human life.

Armour Tests

It was quickly concluded that the armour on the Il-10 was, in fact, far too heavy and posed a serious impediment to performance. Initial tests with a lighter armour, which the Navy shot full of holes at the Dahlgren Proving Ground in Maryland, indicated that any armour of lesser weight was going to provide inadequate protection.

In due course, specifically for the Skyraider, Douglas was able to develop a duraluminum armour package which would better protect the pilot at his back (his six o'clock position) and underneath while adding only about 400 lb (181 kg) to the overall weight of the aircraft. Tests showed that a .50-calibre (12.7-mm) bullet would not penetrate this duraluminium plate unless fired at pointblank range. An explosive 20-mm cannon shell might penetrate but its velocity would be so impeded that it would inflict little or no damage.

It was not easy to 'sell' the idea of a costly modification to an aircraft which had proven itself in battle and was needed, now, without further delays on the production line. Hank Suerstedt felt the selling job was necessary. Suerstedt had gotten in on the tail end of World War 2 and had vivid memories of fighting in the Pacific in a Grumman TBF Avenger which was lightly armoured. In future wars—he seems to have been prescient—the situation would not tolerate inadequate protection for the pilot.

As the 'class desk officer' for the AD Skyraider at the Main Navy Building in Washington, Suerstedt embarked on a public relations campaign within the Navy and, in due course, was able to persuade higher-ups to authorize the improved armour. The AD-6 came off the production line with it and some earlier Skyraiders were retrofitted.

For a time, it appeared that this improvement was going to be available to the Navy but not to the

The city of Oakland, California sprawling beneath them in the 26 September 1958 sunshine, a division of AD-6 Skyraiders of the 'Golden Dragons' of VA-196 demonstrates the grey-white paint scheme. Oakland is adjacent to NAS Alameda, one of the first Skyraider bases (via Hal Andrews)

In December 1960, four AD-6 Skyraiders of the 'Sunday Punchers' of attack squadron VA-75 loiter over the Atlantic, flying from USS Independence (CVA-62). In this final month of the Eisenhower presidency, a few similar AD-6s had already reached South Vietnam (USN)

RIGHT
Performing a little BFM (basic fighter manoeuvring), A-1H (former AD-6) Skyraider 139636, side number AJ-501, of the 'Black Falcons' of VA-85 banks to port. 1950s and 1960s were the heyday of US naval aviation markings, with all manner of special unit designs appearing on aircraft (USN via Peter B Mersky)

USS Intrepid *(CVA-11)
points into the wind on 10
January 1961 as one
Skyraider (at left)
launches and a second
prepares to head into the
air. Aircraft belong to the
'Tigers' of VA-65, home-
ported at NAS Oceana,
Virginia (USN via Peter
B Mersky)*

Marine Corps. It took further effort to persuade the Corps and to get the duraluminium protective fit on all Skyraiders. In later years when the air defence environment in a new Asian country became particularly nasty, pilots were grateful for this feature which evolved continuously over the Skyraider's service career.

Flying the Skyraider with the Fleet was an adventuresome and exciting experience. The naval aviator might not advertise it, but he was a member of an elite breed—proud to be flying from carrier decks and a little pigheaded in his support for his own airplane. Being a naval aviator also meant sacrifice—a typical cruise aboard a carrier might take a pilot away from home for six to seven months—but that came with the turf.

James D Burden, now a retired US Navy captain

End of a Skyraider. On 2 October 1956, AD-6 number 139761, piloted by LTJG Folta of VA-16, made this spectacular crackup aboard USS Lake Champlain *(CVA-38). The fate of the pilot is not on record (USN via Peter B Mersky)*

RIGHT
USS Coral Sea *(CVA-43) underneath, AD-6 Skyraider 134605, side number NL-203, of squadron VA-152 wings its way over Pacific waters on 22 March 1961. Six months later, the aircraft was redesignated A-1H (USN)*

employed by Tracor Flight Systems, is typical of the naval aviators of the 1950s who spent virtually an entire career—including wars in Korea and Vietnam—flying the Skyraider.

Interview Subject

'From the horse's mouth.' That's American slang for the straight story from the real source. The following interview with Captain Jim Burden is presented verbatim, as the words were spoken, to give readers a feel for the Skyraider direct from a lifelong pilot of the aircraft. Before moving directly to the pilot's words, it should be added that Jim Burden is an exceedingly quiet and modest man—and a lucky one. In heavy fighting in two wars while flying the

Skyraider, he proved to be a genuine hero. He also managed to escape serious harm or injury. In fact, the worst incident that Burden ever experienced was a peacetime fire aboard a T-2 Buckeye, an aircraft he flew only occasionally.

In Burden's own words:
My first impressions of the airplane? It was a good airplane, a forgiving airplane, an honest airplane.

I went through advanced training in the F4U-4 Corsair. The first Fleet squadron we reported to was then called VA-74 at Quonset Point. Rhode Island in December 1949. The skipper was Bill Morton. He was a holdover World War 2 guy, very much decorated, a hard-fighting, hard-drinking guy. Had to grip his coffee with two hands in the morning! He was relieved by a guy named Nils Larsen, who was very conservative by comparison.

[Morton] took off on one flight of sixteen airplanes. Four divisions. And he forgot to raise his landing gear. We

didn't know what to do. We raised ours but he flew the airplane so damned slow with the gear down we didn't know how to keep up with him. So as we reached the field we got into the break and he was ready to land. He reached to put his gear down and discovered, of course, that it was already down!

The squadron was subsequently redesignated VA-75. It was called the 'Sunday Punchers'. You may have seen their insignia which was a bomb being held by boxing gloves. It later became an A-6 [Grumman Intruder] squadron.

I showed up in December of '49 at Quonset Point. The squadron had F4U-4s. And they transitioned then into the Skyraider. During that period, Louis Johnson was the Secretary of Defense and he was really cutting back on the budget. What I remember most vividly about that was that money was so damned tight, we were supposed to go aboard ship early in 1950. We were scheduled for it. And of course none of us had seen the airplane before. And as a budget measure, the old-timers in the squadron were limited to four hours' flying time per month so that we could get ten hours in order to qualify for the carrier. That's not very much flying, only ten hours, when you want to learn a new airplane and take it on the carrier.

That was interesting. I remember my first take-off in a Skyraider. In fact, I was with Joe Reyes, who became an old friend of mine. We took off from Quonset, first flight in the bird. They'd turned us loose and we felt ready to handle it. I think the thing that impressed me the most was that bird's climbing ability. It got up to 10,000 feet [3048 m] before you hardly knew you were off the ground. It was very remarkable compared to the rate of climb of the Corsair.

I think this was the AD-2 version we were flying in those days. In that squadron we eventually flew AD-3s and AD-4s. I later on flew the AD-1s but that was with Training Command. I think I've flown every version of the Skyraider, with a considerable amount of time spent in the AD-6, but the first one in those days was the AD-2.

Skyraider Baptism

To return to that first flight that Joe Reyes and I took in the bird—this was, of course, two of us in two single-seat Skyraiders—basically they said, 'Well, here it is, guys.' We had read the handbook so we said, 'Okay' and took the handle and they just turned us loose.

The weather closed in on us and we were of course milling around all over the place. We were around the port and the bridges at Quonset Point. The weather closed in and we eventually got back by going back out to sea and coming in under the bridge. You know, the bridge that goes across the Jamestown River at Quonset Point. It's a very high bridge. Nobody ever actually accused us of flying under the bridge but later on over the bar we allowed as how that was a pretty interesting first flight in the bird. We got interviewed by the CAG [commander, air group] when we got back, too, because we were late. People were asking,

The 'Sunday Punchers' of VA-75 were later selected to introduce the Grumman A-6A Intruder to combat in Southeast Asia. In 1960, however, the NAS Oceana, Virginia squadron's medium attack aircraft was the AD-6 Skyraider, shown here during operations aboard USS Independence *(CVA-62) (USN via Peter B Mersky)*

125

TOP
*Training mission. 135267
(3T-118) and 135279
(3T-119) belong to
training squadron VT-30
at NAS Corpus Christi,
Texas. The two AD-6
Skyraiders are seen flying
through Texas skies on 22
August 1961* (USN via
Peter B Mersky)

LEFT
*Out west somewhere,
possibly at NAS Fallon,
Nevada, AD-6 Skyraider
139633, side number NK-
406, is being loaded with
practice rounds for bomb
drops out on the range.
Black streaking from
R-3350 engine is
particularly evident
around rear of cowling*
(USN via Peter B
Mersky)

In July 1961, an AD-6 Skyraider moves up on the deck of USS Forrestal *(CVA-59) to be spotted. F8U-1 Crusader is in background* (USN via Peter B Mersky)

'Where are those two new ensigns who just reported aboard and why aren't they back?'

About the sequence of events that led to our going to Korea in the AD Skyraider, VA-74 which, as I said a little later on was redesignated VA-75, made several deployments in 1950 along the east coast on the carrier *Leyte* [CVA-32] and others. In 1950, we also went to the Mediterranean aboard the carrier *Midway* [CVA-41], which was a straight-deck ship at the time. And I think the air wing [actually, the term was carrier air group (CVG) in 1950] was a Skyraider squadron, an F4U squadron, and I think two F9F-2 Panther Deuce squadrons.

So, we came back from that, and what were we doing in 1951? We actually went to Korea in 1952. It was more of the same in 1951, small cruises with the Skyraider. We came back from a deployment and were sent cross-country to pick up the *Bon Homme Richard* [CVA-31] out of San Diego.

So the Air Group then, from about May to December 1952, was deployed aboard *Bon Homme Richard* in the Korean War. The CO was Captain Paul Watson and the exec was Commander Lew Bower. As for the composition of the Air Group, VF-74 had F4U-4s, VF-71 and VF-72 had Panther Deuces, and there were detachments, VC-33 and VC-4. I was still with VA-75, with Skyraiders.

We were very impressed. I think the first targets we were assigned in Korea in May 1952 were the hydroelectric plants. They had not yet been struck as of that part of the war. We got a lot of fireworks on that because of electricity and the bombs hitting the plant and the explosions and so forth.

We ran into quite a bit of flak on the powerplant raid, surprisingly so. Maybe they were expecting us. Anyway, it was a relatively high-value target. We had several airplanes hit but I don't recall us losing any on that particular raid. On subsequent missions we did lose people. We lost the CO [commanding officer] of the squadron during our last week but that wasn't near the front lines, that was down near the DMZ. It was near the demarcation line which later became the DMZ. There was very heavy small-arms fire. They told us to watch out at [an altitude of] 4000 or 3500 feet. He was just about down there amongst them when he got hit. This was the skipper of VA-75 we lost, LCDR Al Evans.

In 1952, we had straight AD-4s although some squadrons had what was known as the Queen version or AD-4Q with a guy sitting in back. That was the latest they had so they gave those to us. Now, squadron VC-33 which was the night detachment for night and all-weather attack was equipped with the Queens, the AD-4Qs. Later on in a different period we had some in our squadron too but we began our deployment with just the straight AD-4s.

One thing I remember about the Korean War which sort of irritated me and, I think, a bunch of other guys at the time too, was this: We were briefed for a mock invasion [he is discussing the pilots' unhappiness that they were asked to take heavy risks to support a planned amphibious landing which never took place] cutting off the peninsula north of the Wonsan area. We were so briefed on it that we were

Aboard USS Intrepid *(CVA-11) on 10 January 1961, AD-6 Skyraiders of the 'Tigers' of VA-65 are directed to the catapult. Aircraft in background is 137607, side number NF-400 (USN via Peter B Mersky)*

In this four-ship formation, an A-1J (former AD-7) 142076, side number NH-502, flies division lead ahead of three similar A-1H (former AD-6) aeroplanes. The aircraft belong to the 'Arabs' of VA-115 and are operating from USS Kitty Hawk *(CVA-63) on 15 July 1965 (USN)*

strafing down at the treetops and exposing ourselves to some rather significant degree. And Walt Alt, one of the guys in the squadron, got shot down—right there in the middle of Wonsan harbour.

Walt got shot down by small-calibre guns. We were very low. We were strafing troop emplacements and he got hit. He did a very good ditching job in the harbour. A helicopter picked him up and took him ashore south of the front lines so that he was in friendly territory. But it was some time before he actually got back to the squadron. Walt got back in one piece but in the process he witnessed a lot of brutality in the ground fighting and came back with some pretty wild stories.

Ditching at Sea

What do you do in an AD when you know you'll have to ditch it? You want to make it very similar to a landing appraoch except that you need your wheels up. We of course practiced that at altitude where we couldn't hurt ourselves. You want to get the airplane in a dirty configuration with the flaps down but with the gear up, canopy open, and into the wind. We always figured that the safest way to get out of that bird, among the options—if the sea state wasn't too severe—was to ditch it.

If you ditched it, you'd probably be okay—if there was somebody to pull you out of the water. But you know, bailing out of the thing was another matter. Bailing out of the Skyraider, a lot of guys hit the horizontal stabilizer. So we all were reluctant to go that route if we could help it. More than that, if you were over land and in trouble you'd try to make it to a field or try to land on a road rather than bail out of the airplane.

And of course there was the new AD-5 version which was side-by-side. We didn't have that in Korea.

I think the raid I remember most from the Korean War was the one on Pyongyang, which was 11 August 1952. We had a two-group strike, ourselves from the *Bon Homme Richard* and also the group from the *Princeton*.

We must have had twenty-odd airplanes shot up and a couple shot down, so you do have to pay a price. We were under heavy and concentrated anti-aircraft fire all the way from Yangdok, which is halfway across the peninsula, until we got to the target.

We were hitting various targets in the Pyongyang area— airfield, railroad yards, some industrial plants. We put in two full deckloads, ourselves and *Princeton*'s, and we had— let's see—eight planes from my squadron, eight more from our ship, and the fighters carried some ordnance too, so it was about sixty airplanes total. We didn't use the term Alpha Strike in those days but the force consisted of F4U Corsairs flying CAP [combat air patrol] and carrying bombs, too, and our principal fighter escort was the F9F-2 Panthers. They also carried bombs too but not many, I think six 250s [113-kg]. The F4Us would probably carry two 1000 pounders [454-kg] or a single 2000-pounder

[908-kg] and maybe a couple of 250s [113-kg] on the wings. The Skyraider, of course, carried everything up to and including the kitchen sink that somebody dropped on the North Koreans.

We did a lot of bombing on railroads, too. I remember there was a *Time* magazine 'before' and 'after' shot that showed a railroad turntable. We hit that roundhouse and turntable pretty well with 2000-lb [454-kg] bombs.

In later years of course I felt the AD-6 was the optimum Skyraider. I went through my whole career in the AD and flew the Skyraider in two wars without ever realizing that it had been designed in a hotel room!

I made deployments on the *Philippine Sea* [CVA-47] off the Atlantic coast. We had some guys in Skyraiders who claimed to have made a landing on board almost every carrier in the Fleet! Beyond question, we did get around a lot in those days.

What was it like to be a naval aviator in the AD-6 in the fifties? What comes back to mind? When we were going through flight training with this airplane we learned to watch out for the canopy with the manual hand crank. The

Spad had a 3000-lb [1360-kg] hydraulic system, so when we went flying with our long white scarves flying in the breeze and put that lever forward in the Skyraider, we could get in trouble. One of the guys just about got strangled before he got back to base! So we sort of got away from wearing the white scarves!

As to our attitude towards flying with the canopy open, this varied over time. We started out with the airplane in the early days taking off from shore or from the carrier with the canopy open. Later on, probably about the time we got into the newer AD-6 model, we kind of changed out thoughts on the canopy, deciding that at night, especially, if it was pretty noisy, it was easier to hear the controller with the canopy shut. On a night approach to the carrier you want to be doggoned sure you hear what somebody's telling you. Early on, our thinking had been that if you had problems [at low altitude near the carrier] having the canopy open would help you to get out of the airplane.

PRECEDING PAGES AND THESE PAGES
A-1H Skyraider 135300 (NL-405) of the 'Fist of the Fleet' on USS Coral Sea (CVA-43) was chosen for ceremonies to mark retirement of the combat Skyraider from the Fleet. On 10 April 1968, ship 405 taxies in for the occasion at NAS Lemoore, California. Subsequently, this Skyraider reached the US Navy Museum at NAS Pensacola, Florida, where it is seen on 12 November 1974 (distant view) and 13 April 1975 (close-up) (US Navy)

On the Boat

A carrier landing in the AD-6? Early on, we did not have the landing signal mirror. It was strictly an LSO approach.

Normally, we would be coming across the ship and would drop the gear as we crossed the landing area. We would break off, bank, and drop the gear and flaps. If you were going fast enough you might also want to extend the speed brakes to help slow down. On downwind, of course, we had gear and flaps down. So we came around the downwind leg and we were at about 125 ft [38 m] and that's when we turned at the 180 and tried to have, at that time, a speed of about 88 knots, give or take a knot or two. We tried to keep that speed coming around. We made a rounded approach into the final.

So you're now at about 100 ft [305 m] and you gradually work that down. It was pretty much a nose-high approach without power. The LSO on the ship [landing signal officer] didn't want you low in the groove because it was hard to see you. And from your point of view it was hard to see the deck and to see him, so he didn't want to have you disappearing unexpectedly. The LSO was using manual signals. He had his paddles out there. If you were high, he would indicate high. If you were low, he would [signal you]. If you were fast, he'd drop one paddle. If you were slow, he'd give you a come-on signal. And if he didn't like what he saw he'd just wave you off with his two paddles over his head.

We did have voice communication with the LSO as well. He'd give you additional things about power, or, 'Watch your nose!' Of course, sometimes if you had radio failure you were strictly on visual with the paddles.

On a landing, without power and relatively flat, in a

three-point attitude, the LSO would bring you in as close as he could—think back to during the Korean thing, when we still had a straight deck on our aircraft carriers—and we liked to shoot for the number two or number three wire. The number one wire was a little bit chancy in case the deck was moving. And you didn't want to get too far down or you might hit that barrier, the barricade. So we thought you were in a good position if you could catch that number two or three wire. And if the LSO thought so, he would give you a cut. It was a cutting-type signal—at which point you would just chop off all the power, drop the nose slightly, start a rate of descent and then come back to a three-point attitude, and hopefully you would engage the wire. Because if you didn't, before we had the angled deck if you didn't catch the wire you went into the barricade. You would just smash into the airplanes [parked on deck] forward.

The AD-5 with the wide-body came along after the Korean War. I flew that model. I didn't care that much for it, and I think most people didn't, because it was so heavy and it was a wallowy type of bird. You had to keep a lot of power on it, for landing for example. If you took the power off the whole bottom would drop out, it was so heavy. As I said, in later yeas I flew the AD-6 model for more than a decade and that was the best.

I stayed with the same squadron for a long time. I was with VA-75 from December 1949 until around Christmas 1952. I reported after the Holidays, at the beginning of 1953, down to Advanced Training Command [ATU]. I instructed in both F6s and AD Skyraiders at Corpus [Christi, Texas], at Cabiness Field, and they had [older] AD-1s down there. They had the F6F-5s, the Hellcat, and they had the AD-1s. They tended to concentrate the AD-1s there in the training command.

Skyraider Training

How do you teach someone to fly the AD Skyraider? You can't sit behind him and watch. You try to get in as much as you can beforehand, in ground school and going around the ready room and talking to him. But for flying, it has to be one-on-one, so you try to get the new pilot to get a feel for the airplane so that he can go up and try it out, try the low speed characteristics, simulate landing gear problems and then come back to the field . . . and of course we'd have what we called FAM officers. It stands for familiarization. They'd be like an LSO, they'd be out there on the runway with a radio and coach the guy around for his first landing or his first series of landings. The first time out, he might make as many as ten landings depending on how the FAM officer thought he was doing.

The FAM officer was a king of a ground-based instructor. We would give them a little air work first and then bring them back and have the FAM officer work them through landing techniques. You figured that once he learned how to land and take off the airplane you could go on to other things, like flying in formation, tactics, gunnery, and bombing.

Skyraider Students

Our student pilots came to us from NAS Pensacola, Florida, from primary training in the SNJ. At Corpus Christi they came for training in one of the single-engine Fleet airplanes, at Cabiness Field for training in the F6F or Skyraider, or at Chaee Field or Beeville for F9F-2 Panthers or [twin-engine] Banshees.

They started from the beginning by making their first solo in the AD and gradually moved up to gunnery and bombing. Normally, once you got them past the FAM stage you would get them into a flight, and that would be seven or eight airplanes and the instructor would bring up the rear. The instructor would rotate the lead around so that each student would get practice in leading the flight and, of course, practice rendevous. And of course being in the rear of the flight was also the safest place for an instructor to be, if you had students on the dangerous side! You'd feel a little more comfortable critiquing them from out in back than you would if you were up front and they were bunching up on you!

Once my training assignment was up, late in 1955 I reported to USS *Intrepid* (CVA-11), first as arresting gear officer and then as flight deck officer. That was based out of Norfolk. After I reported aboard, *Intrepid* went back into the shipyard for the angled-deck conversion. *Intrepid* also got the Mark 7 arresting gear. She got the angled deck and

On 18 September 1962, the US system for designating military aircraft went through a major change. The AD-6 became the A-1H. Soon thereafter, a new war made itself felt to Americans. The 'Thunderbolts' of VA-176 were an east coast/Atlantic Fleet squadron but when this view of A-1H Skyraider 139609 was taken, they were in combat in South Vietnam (via Dave Ostrowski)

the steam catapults. Earlier, carriers had had hydraulic catapults, the H-4 and the H-8, and they gave you a really quick, hard shot compared to the newer and better steam cats. The steam cat would accelerate you the whole length of the cat track, which was 120 ft [36 m]. The hydraulic cat would only accelerate you for the first one-third or so of that distance, with a real severe kick in the back. The steam catapult had much more capability as far as payload and the end speed.

One interesting sidelight was that on *Intrepid* we had a fighter squadron of F7Us [Vought Cutlasses]. Anyway, I flew the AD-6 on *Intrepid* until 1957 when I went back to school. In 1959, I reported to attack squadron VA-52 at NAS Miramar, California, also flying the AD-6. The squadron was known as the 'Knight Riders' and we deployed on the USS *Ticonderoga* (CVA-14)—twice.

By this time the aircraft were painted grey and white. This was a major change in American naval aviation history. The change may have had to do with the mission of the airplane—long range delivery of nuclear weapons, where the blue colour obviously might stand out more over land. We were never quite sure of the exact reason for the change but clearly they decided that blue wasn't the best way to go.

The thing I remember most about VA-52—the skipper was Al Taddeo, terrific guy—was that we were at the O Club at Yokosuka [Japan] and, as usual, they sent the youngest ensign up to get the squadron flag. In Japan at that time you could get a real bargain having a VA-52 flag made up at a tailor shop in the town. The ensign was sent ashore to see a tailor and show him what the squadron flag looked like, show him our colours, and say that we wanted a flag, which had to be heroic in size so we could use it for ceremonies, such as change-of-command ceremonies. So the young ensign proudly did as he was told and walked up to Al Taddeo and said, 'Skipper, here's the flag!' Our neighbouring squadron saw this and it turned out to be the biggest free-for-all you've ever seen! The other squadron was determined to snatch our flag away from us and we were equally bound and determined not to give it up. Everyone from the CO on down was rolling around and tussling on the floor.

At this point there was not another AD-6 squadron on our ship. The squadron wrestling us for the flag was an AD outfit from another carrier. One thing I remember about that tussle is an admiral turning to our skipper and saying, 'Al, is this really necessary?'

In the 1959–60 time frame, the average composition of a carrier air wing meant that you had one AD-6 Skyraider squadron on the ship. The fighters were Banshees. We sometimes had an FJ squadron too, FJ Furys, and we were the only propeller-driven squadron. I was with VA-52 on *Ticonderoga* from 1959 to about 1961. I went back to school in 1961 and in 1963–65 I was in Washington, in the Navy's Bureau of Personnel. I kept flying all that time, of course.

In 1965, I went back to NAS Lemoore, California and spent a year in the RAG squadron [Replacement Air Group], the 'Flying Eagles' of VA-122. I was operations officer and later executive officer. Now we were flying the AD-6 but it had been redesignated A-1H. I then went to squadron VA-25, the 'Fist of the Fleet', first as exec and then as CO. [Burden commanded VA-25 flying A-1H Skyraiders in combat in Vietnam, his second war in the aircraft].

Navigating

One thing about flying Skyraiders in the 1950s whether it was the early days or later in the AD-6 and AD-7, we always had to think about the weather. We were very vulnerable to bad weather because we had very little in the way of navigational gear. We had one ARC-5 radio receiver which would give you a dah-dit if you were in the A quadrant and a dit-dah if you were in the N quadrant. That's pretty rudimentary for navigation, especially with a lot of crackling in the earphones and in an airplane where you have a lot of background noise. And you couldn't fly an instrument approach to a field on that kind of equipment. It was pretty basic.

I can recall in the winter months fighting the weather many times on cross-countries that I made from Quonset Point to Akron, Ohio, where there was a young lady I wanted to marry. One reason we got married, I think, was when we rationalized that we'd better get hitched before I killed myself navigating in the Skyraider!

I remember more than once the squadron being up in a 'group grope' of twelve to sixteen airplanes and, as it has a habit of doing, the weather would move in there in a hurry. And we couldn't come in like you do today on instrument approaches, so the whole group would mill around looking for a hole in the clouds somewhere and dive down. We would come in between factory smoke stacks or whatever, and . . . it could be a pretty dangerous, hair-raising-type operation. We were just lucky we didn't lose people.

Atom Bomber

The preceding brings the Burden interview to an end. Naval aviators like Jim Burden rarely talked about—and many scarcely knew about—the capability of their aircraft to carry nuclear weapons. Only recently, largely through the efforts of researcher Chuck Hansen, have a few details about the atomic bombs of the era become known.

The AD-4B, AD-6 and AD-7 were supposedly able to carry the Mark 7 atomic warhead either as a free-fall bomb or in the form of a BOAR (Bureau of Ordnance Atomic Rocket). The Mark 8 weapon, itself barely more than an improvement over the *Little Boy* U235 gun-assembly bomb dropped on Hiroshima, was also cleared to be carried by the Skyraider. The latter, also known as *Elsie*, was called the TX-8 in test form. *Elsie* weighed 1700 lb (771 kg) and was stockpiled in the US arsenal beginning in July 1952.

In truth, although the nuclear capabilities of a variety of US warplanes were touted in the 1950s, almost no aircraft in active service could carry a 'nuke' (the term was not in use then) only with extensive modifications. It is not at all clear whether these modifications could have been carried out in the field or aboard a carrier. The TX-8 nuclear 'shape' could be carried externally by an AD-6 only with a T-28 saddle device rigged to its bomb rack.

The Navy, of course, was anxious to retain a nuclear role (in the era which preceeded the submarine-launched ballistic missile) and undertook all manner of activity to keep its hand in. Carriers in the 1950s carried P2V-3C Neptunes which could take off from shipboard with nuclear bombs but could not *land* after completing a mission. Navy strategists routinely assumed that nuclear-armed aircraft would be able to strike Soviet targets from carrier decks. As if to make the point that a mission as vital as delivering atomic bombs should never be left to such an upstart as the US Air Force, a standard Navy map of the 1950s assumed that carriers would be able to operate even in the Black Sea and Caspian Sea!

Although it has always been US policy to neither confirm nor deny the existence of nuclear weapons aboard ship or anywhere else, it is a plain fact that most naval aviators have never seen a nuclear weapon and would not recognize one if they did. In the late 1950s—when the US and the Soviet Union seemed to be in a contest to see who could explode the biggest bomb in the atmosphere—these awesome weapons were very much on peoples' minds. But as will be seen, the Skyraider still had plenty of work ahead involving conventional ordnance.

By the early 1960s, the idea of replacing the Skyraider—a subject which kept coming up prematurely—was now coming close to reality with Grumman developing the A-6 Intruder for the carrier-based medium attack role. It was inevitable that the Fleet would move towards an all-jet force, if only to spare aircraft carriers having to stock different fuels. First flown on 19 April 1960 and known at the time as the A2F-1, the Intruder seemed to show real promise. In fact, years of developmental work would be needed before the promise could be redeemed.

In the meanwhile, as there always is, there remained one more war to be fought.

Chapter 7
AD-7
The Spad in the Dragon's Den

When the AD-7 version of the Skyraider (later known as A-1J) was delivered it had the distinction of being the first variant to come straight from the Douglas factory not in sea gloss blue but in the mid-1950s gray and white paint scheme. Apart from that, the single-seat AD-7 which began its production run with aeroplane 142010 was litttle different from its AD-6 predecessor. It introduced structural strengthening in the wings, fuselage and landing gear, and not much else that was different.

For a time in the late 1950s it appeared that the Skyraider production line might keep going forever. The Navy clearly wanted to obtain more AD-7s than, in the end, it actually acquired. The Marine Corps, which ceased operating the Skyraider when squadron VMA-331 at MCAS Iwakuni, Japan dispensed with its final machine in 1959, never really accepted no longer possessing an aircraft which continued to be the principal medium attack asset on carrier decks.

In the end, two batches of 84 aircraft, each in the AD-7 series were cancelled. Those who worked on, flew—and loved—the Skyraider would never accept it, but the jet age had finally finished arriving. 18 February 1957, as it turned out, was the date of rollout of the last piston-engine combat aircraft manufactured in the United States, when gray/white AD-7 Skyraider 142081 came off the line at El Segundo. 142081 was the 3180th Skyraider and was delivered to the 'Barn Owls' of VA-215 at NAS Moffett Field, California.

Another milestone was passed in 1956 when a Skyraider made the last landing on a straight-deck carrier. The angled deck was now standard throughout the Fleet. Vessel for the final such landing was the USS *Lake Champlain* (CVA-39).

On 18 September 1962, the Pentagon changed its system for designating military aircraft. The legend has grown that Secretary of Defense Robert S McNamara testified about aircraft purchases before Congress without realizing that the Navy and Air Force used different systems for designating their aircraft. In fact, there is no written record of such testimony. But for whatever reason, a unified, all-service system was adopted.

The changes were as follows:
AD-4 became A-1D
AD-5 became A-1E
AD-5W became EA-1E
AD-5Q became EA-1F
AD-5N became A-1G
AD-6 became A-1H
AD-7 became A-1J

Contrary to some published reports, the designations A-1A through A-1C were *not* assigned.

The change in nomenclature took some time to absorb—a few people were bitter about the Navy having to give up its traditional system for naming airplanes, and a few still feel that way today. But as war clouds gathered on the horizon, the Skyraider also won another appellation from a new generation of warriors. The Spad, it became. The nickname was partly a word play on the obsolete AD designation and partly a reference to the World War 1 fighter of the same name—so ancient did the Skyraider seem in a jet era.

New War

The Douglas Skyraider—Spad, it will be called interchangeably from this point onward—fought the American war in Southeast Asia from beginning to end and was in the air, still fighting, on 30 April 1975—the day Saigon was evacuated.

If the fall of Saigon marked a sad and bitter end, the beginning occurred in September 1960 when the first US naval officer in combat, Lieutenant Ken Moranville, arrived at Bien Hoa to familiarize

LEFT
The final version of the Skyraider to fly in combat from carrier decks, EA-1F (former AD-5Q) of early warning squadron VAW-33 cranks up aboard USS Intrepid *(CVS-11) in the Gulf of Tonkin on 18 September 1967 (USN)*

ABOVE
As seen from an HU-16B Albatross amphibian on a search and rescue (SAR) mission, an A-1H Skyraider (134515) from USS Ticonderoga *(CVA-19) prowls the Gulf of Tonkin. Side number NM-304 belongs to the 'Knight Riders' of VA-52 and carries only fuel, ammo and cluster bomb units (USAF)*

USS Shangri-La *(CVA-38) acquired an angled deck in the
mid-1950s but remained ancient by contemporary
standards. This 20 November 1960 view shows Skyraiders
lined up on* Shang's *wooden deck. During the Vietnam
conflict, the carrier took on the anti-submarine mission and
became CVS-38* (USN)

Another typical shipboard view shows steam wafting upward from the powerful catapults aboard USS Forrestal (CVA-59) on 1 March 1963. A-1H Skyraider 135323 (side number AJ-500) belongs to the 'Black Falcons' of VA-85 (USN)

Vietnamese Air Force (VNAF) pilots with the single-seat Skyraider—still known, then, as the AD-6 but soon to become the A-1H. That month, at the airfield a few miles northeast of Saigon, the VNAF's 1st Fighter Squadron (redesignated 514th Fighter Squadron on 1 January 1963) received the first six of a batch of twenty-four AD-6 Skyraiders, offloaded in Saigon by the jeep carrier USS *Core* and trucked to Bien Hoa. The AD-6 was then the standard medium attack aircraft in the US Fleet, but the airplanes being turned over to the Vietnamese would have been the envy of many an American sailor.

Once their preservative was removed at Bien Hoa, the AD-6s looked pristine. Painted in the standard US Navy scheme of light gull grey (FS-595a colour 36440) on top and insignia white (colour 17875) underneath, the AD-6s had been rebuilt at the Naval Air Rework Facility (NARF), North Island, California at a cost of 5250 man-hours and $133,000 per aircraft. No fewer than a dozen US Navy carrier squadrons were operating the Skyraider, which had begun life as a replacement for the World War 2 SBD Dauntless, but the 'newest' and best airplanes of the type now belonged to the Vietnamese.

The gradually expanding VNAF was seeking to bring airpower to bear on an elusive enemy, the Viet Cong guerrilla who fought in rural areas and small towns, lived among the population, and controlled, the small but growing Vietnam war after dark. Fast jets did not seem suitable for pressing the conflict to the scattered but determined Viet Cong. The A-1H (and almost identical A-1J) Skyraider operated by the VNAF could linger in the air over ground troops, follow them on 'search and destroy' missions, and remain overhead while a ground battle unfolded. The Skyraider was also remarkably accurate, not because it possessed any 'magic' black boxes but because it could fight 'down in the weeds' where the infantrymen were. The Skyraider pilot's war was far from impersonal as he saw the enemy at close range ever day.

The availability of the Skyraider transformed the VNAF, theretofore equipped with Grumman F8F Bearcats, from an occasional flying entity to genuine air force. Twenty-two of the AD-6s were in inventory by January 1962, the month the VNAF logged 251 combat sorties in the type. American advisors who followed Moranville found themselves in a land seething with political intrigue—there were six coup attempts and two assassinations between 1960 and 1965—but when they were permitted to concentrate

The hornet emblem used by the 'Thunderbolts' of VA-176 became a familiar sight in Vietnamese skies even though the unit was officially an east coast squadron. A-1H Skyraider 137496 (side number AK-405) belonging to LCDR W N Zimmerman is operating from the deck of USS Intrepid *(CVS-11) (USN)*

on flying they had only one real complaint.

Under the rules, the Americans could not participate in combat. When the A-1E (and similar A-1G) with side-by-side seating became available to the VNAF, a Vietnamese national had to be on board if a combat mission took place. This sometimes meant a skilled American pilot in command and a fledgling Vietnamese who was, in truth, little more than a passenger.

Gulf of Tonkin Strikes

On 5 August 1964, the US launched naval air strikes against torpedo boat installations and POL (petroleum oil lubricant) storage in North Vietnam in retaliation for attacks in the Tonkin Gulf on two of its destroyers. In the 'Gulf of Tonkin air strikes', A-1H and A-1J Skyraiders went into action from squadrons VA-52 ('Knight Riders') and VA-145 ('Swordsmen'), from the carriers *Ticonderoga* (CVA-14) and *Constellation* (CVA-64) respectively. The best-known casualty was an A-4 Skyhawk pilot who became the first prisoner of war (POW) casualty, but the A-1 Skyraider community suffered, too. VA-145's Lieutenant James S Hardie was hit by anti-aircraft fire and managed to limp back to a safe recovery aboard *Constellation*. VA-52's Lieutenant Richard Sather, pilot of A-1H Skyraider 139760 was hit and went down—the first American lost in combat over North Vietnam.

A-1E Skyraider 132417 of the First Air Commando Squadron carrying napalm and rockets over Southeast Asia. When the US Air Force began operating these Skyraiders, initially with the 34th Tactical Group at Bien Hoa, they retained their Navy-style overall paint scheme. This early view was probably taken in 1964 (USAF)

RIGHT
Listed as a 'VNAF A-1E' in the caption prepared in Saigon (by the same public affairs office which held a daily briefing known as the Five O'Clock Follies), this Skyraider attacking Viet Cong positions in 1965 is almost certainly being flown by a US Air Force, rather than Vietnamese Air Force, pilot (USAF via R J Mills, Jr)

US Navy carrier-based Skyraiders had a key role in the first major search and rescue effort of the war on 18–19 November 1964. It began when BALL 3, one of two F-100 Super Sabres escorting a reconnaissance mission over Laos, was shot down while trading fire with a communist anti-aircraft gun position. Several rescue aircraft converged on the scene including a Grumman HU-16B Albatross amphibian functioning as an airborne command post and using the callsign TACKY 44. The Albatross requested US Navy A-1E Skyraiders to fly to the Ban Senphan area to join the search for F-100 wreckage and pilot.

Arriving overhead, the Skyraiders were engaged by AAA (anti-aircraft artillery) batteries. They

attacked the gun positions with cluster bombs and 20-mm fire, while searching in vain for the downed F-100 pilot. The Skyraiders then linked up with rescue helicopters and escorted them. Because of communications problems a rescue attempt was not possible until the following day when the body of the F-100 pilot was recovered where he had died of injuries from his ejection. Even without success, an important precedent had been set: it had been demonstrated that the Skyraider was the ideal aircraft to escort rescue helicopters behind enemy lines.

As a user of the Skyraider in the conflict, behind the VNAF and the US Navy came the US Air Force, which went to war in Southeast Asia almost as if to reconstruct the mood and flavour of World War 2. Air Commandos from Hurlburt Field in the Florida panhandle flew in support of their South Vietnamese ally in B-26, T-28 and C-123 aircraft, ostensibly as advisors but in fact participating in combat so long as a requisite Vietnamese national was present in the airplane.

Problems with both B-26 and T-28 led to the USAF decision to adopt the A-1 Skyraider in 1964. The USAF's 34th Tactical Group, quickly supplanted by the First Air Commando Squadron, went to Bien Hoa airbase to operate the 'wide-body' A-1E (former AD-5). Also in 1964, the USAF took over from the Navy the job of training Vietnamese Skyraider pilots.

As the VNAF expanded (eventually operating no fewer than eight squadrons of Skyraiders), a pilot training programme was established in the US. Vietnamese trainees went to Lackland AFB, Texas, for 15 weeks of language study, stayed for a 42-week basic flight course at nearby Randolph AFB, Texas, then moved to Hurlburt Field for an 18-week schedule which gave them 85 hours of flying time in the A-1E.

In the war zone, the USAF's own airplanes were not all in top condition. Typical was A-1E number 132649, described as 'a dog' by the sergeant who maintained it. On 21 March 1965, 132649 crashed at Can Tho in the Mekong Delta, killing two American captains on board, and official records show the aircraft 'written off' on that date. In fact, 132649 was hitched to a CH-54 Skycrane helicopter and taken back to Saigon's Tan Son Nhut airbase where it flew again.

When President Johnson began the sustained bombing of North Vietnam in February 1965, all three services operating the Skyraider—USAF, US Navy, VNAF—participated. A brilliant leader but also, in the words of his own maintenance chief, a 'very average pilot', Saigon's fiery Nguyen Cao Ky led a Skyraider force north of the 17th Parallel on 2 February 1965, experienced a communications problem, and attacked the wrong target. USAF Air Commandos for the first time were permitted to fly into combat without a Vietnamese accompanying them in the aircraft. Carrier-based US Navy squadrons attacked northern targets from ship decks in the Gulf of Tonkin.

MiG Killer

One such squadron, VA-25, nicknamed 'Fist of the Fleet', operating from USS *Midway* (CVA-41) was covering a rescue attempt on 20 June 1965 when MiG-17s of the still-developing North Vietnamese air arm engaged the A-1H Skyraiders. In a head-to-head encounter, Lieutenants Charlie Hartman and Clinton Johnson in A-1H airplanes 137523 and 139768 fired bursts of 20-mm fire and blew a MiG-17 out of the sky.

A second prop-versus-jet aerial victory was achieved on 9 October 1966 when LTJG William T Patton of the 'Thunderbolts' of VA-176, flying A-1H Skyraider 137543 from USS *Intrepid* (CVS-11) shot down a MiG-17 near Hanoi. The principal accomplishment of the Skyraider, though, was to carry enormous tonnages of ordnance and to remain over the target for marathon duration. Unlike the short-legged, light attack A-4 Skyhawk, the Skyraider could range anywhere in North Vietnam from carrier decks. Once over a target, it would stay and fight. Without air-refuelling capability, pilots routinely flew four- and five-hour missions, always grateful for the spacious cockpit accommodation in the A-1.

In the early days, Skyraiders carried the 'fat', box-finned bombs which remained from World War 2.

This Vietnamese pilot sitting in an AD-6 (future A-1H) at Bien Hoa in October 1960 is one of the first local airmen trained by Skyraider pilot Ken Moranville, the first US Navy officer in action in Southeast Asia. VNAF pilots were trained by the US Navy until about 1964 when the US Air Force took over the job (courtesy Rosario Rausa)

RIGHT
A-1E Skyraider 133885 of First Air Commando Squadron takes off from Bien Hoa in 1965. 'Slick' napalm bombs shown here could not be aimed easily and required pilot to attack at very low level. Finned napalm tanks could be released from higher altitude with a greater degree of accuracy (USAF, via R J Mills Jr)

Gradually, there became available newer, sleeker Mark 82, Mark 83 and Mark 84 bombs weighing 500, 1000 and 2000 lbs (227, 454, and 908 kg) sometimes fitted with Snakeye high-drag fins to retard their fall. Napalm came in finned and unfinned canisters. The variety of other ordnance carried by the Skyraider was too encyclopedic for enumeration here. It ranged from a pod containing nineteen 2.75-in FFAR (folding fin aircraft rocket) projectiles to BLU-52A/B (bomb live unit), a weapon concocted by mixing bulk tear gas with napalm.

It was the 'attack' Skyraider (the single-seat A-1H

and A-1J and the side-by-side A-1E) which carried all manner of bombs and rockets to their Viet Cong and North Vietnamese recipients. But long before the war, the Skyraider had also established a reputation for successfully carrying out a variety of specialized roles. One of these was the airborne early warning (AEW) mission. Typical was Detachment R, squadron VAW-11, which operated five EA-1E (former AD-5W) aircraft from USS *Kearsarge* (CVA-33). On one combat cruise, the squadron flew its Skyraiders operationally for 501 hours, a record. Though the last Navy 'attack' Skyraider was retired from the war zone in July 1968, the EA-1E and similar EA-1F remained in Southeast Asia until September 1968, their duties thereafter taken over by the Grumman EA-1B Tracer.

April 1968, however, marks the 'end' of the Navy Skyraider story as far as many are concerned. It was during April that VA-25, the 'Fist of the Fleet', retired the Navy's very last A-1H/J model in ceremonies at NAS Lemoore, California. LTJG Ted Hill was the last man to fly such an aircraft, bringing in side number NL-405 for the hail and farewell.

Side number NL-405 was in fact aeroplane number 135300 and had also achieved the distinction of flying the last combat mission against North Vietnam from the deck of USS *Coral Sea* (CVA-43).

Thanks to a keen sense of history on the part of many in naval aviation, this last A-1H has been preserved at the Naval Aviation Museum in Pensacola, Florida, and can be viewed on display there today.

Air Force Action

On 10 March 1966, Viet Cong troops laid seige to the Special Forces camp at A Shau. So close were they to overrunning the place, the commander was standing and shooting enemy soldiers in the head with an M-16 rifle. A-1E Skyraiders overhead began delivering ordnance almost within arm's reach of the camp's American and South Vietnamese defenders. Major Dafford W Myers, head of the Qui Nhon detachment of the 602nd Fighter Squadron (Commando) was overhead in aircraft 133867 when VC gunfire sent him crash-landing at the camp's unused runway, littered with rubble and debris. Overhead, Myers' wingman, Major Hubert G King, was also hit, blinded, and forced to leave the area. It looked as if Myers was about to be taken prisoner by VC troops coming through the wire.

Major Bernard G Fisher of the First Air Commando Squadron organized air-to-ground support for Myers, then pulled off a dramatic and

Lt Col Eugene Deatrick took command of the 602nd Special Operations Squadron in 1968 and began to lead A-1 Skyraider missions against the VC and North Vietnamese. Deatrick rescued a Navy Skyraider pilot, Dieter Dengler, who had escaped from the communists in Laos (courtesy Col Deatrick)

astonishing feat. Fisher landed his A-1E Skyraider on the debris-strewn, crater-filled runway with the VC all around. Myers came running and leaped into the A-1E head-first. Fisher rammed his throttle to the firewall and took off under heavy fire. A soft-spoken family man from Kuna, Idaho who did not drink, smoke or swear—scarcely the image of a fighter jock—Bernie Fisher became the first airman to earn the Medal of Honor in Vietnam. Fisher's airplane was number 132649, the same trouble-prone airframe which had killed two captains in Can Tho a year earlier.

Even before Fisher's exploit, the US Air Force managed to devise a new role for the venerable Skyraider. In fits and starts, a wholly new kind of air combat capability was being developed—the capability to penetrate deep into an enemy's homeland and engage his forces solely for the purpose of rescuing airmen downed behind the lines.

Helicopters and support aircraft dedicated to combat rescue required an armed escort and an on-scene commander (OSC). The latter was a heart-rendering job: under fire, deep inside North Vietnam or Laos, the OSC would have to make the decision whether to commit assets to a rescue. If North Vietnamese troops were too close, or ground fire too intense, the OSC had to decide to abandon a countryman to what could become years of imprisonment. If a rescue could be accomplished, Skyraiders

A-1E Skyraider of the First Air Commando Squadron drops unfinned napalm on Viet Cong positions in 1965 (USAF via R J Mills, Jr)

TOP RIGHT
This A-1E Skyraider 133878 pulls away from a phosphorus explosion from its own ordnance. Aircraft has Vietnamese Air Force insignia but probably has a USAF pilot (USAF)

with their formidable ordnance, toughness under fire, and loitering capability could cover it. The rescue escort mission got under way in June 1965, the Skyraiders using the callsign SANDY, the OSC usually being SANDY 1.

Sandy Mission

Eventually, the word Sandy became a generic term for Air Force rescue missions with the Skyraider. On 1 January 1967, the USAF changed the names of its Skyraider squadrons in Southeast Asia to belatedly divest itself of the Air Commando image, which was not popular with the Pentagon brass. Skyraider units became Special Operations Squadrons (SOS). In time, the USAF operated the 1st, 6th, 22nd and

602nd SOS. During 1964–68, these units were moved repeatedly around South Vietnam and Thailand.

A senior USAF official today and potential future Chief of Staff, Lt Gen Michael J Dugan who runs policy and plans for the Air Staff in the Pentagon, accumulated no less than 1700 hours in the A-1 Skyraider and served with the First Air Commando Squadron (later, 1st SOS), then located at Pleiku. To Mike Dugan, the Skyraider was 'a terrible plane for cross-country on a weekend, but great in combat. It had a good load, it loitered, it had good radios [UHV, VHF and HF] all of them, and you could net them with Army FM radios [on the ground, for better coordination on close air support missions].'

On 13 March 1966, Dugan was aloft over Laos in A-1E aircraft 133873. As usual except on check rides, he was flying the side-by-side version of the aircraft solo. He and his wingman were testing one of the Skyraider's encyclopedic repetoire of munitions, in this case the XM-66 small mine, known as 'gravel', intended as an anti-personnel weapon. Apparently Dugan's wingman dropped 'gravel' on him. In any case, Dugan's wing was blown off and he went spiraling downward near the NVA-infested Mu Gia pass, a critical juncture along the infiltration network known as the Ho Chi Minh Trail.

Dugan jettisoned his canopy and, in an inverted attitude, got out of 133873 by the expedient of

releasing his seat-harness and dropping. His .38 pistol was torn from its web belt but his parachute opened normally and his 'beeper' (hand-held radio with voice capability) enabled him to stay in touch. He found the jungle noisy at night. There was construction nearby, hammering. The NVA never learned Dugan was in their midst and at 8.30 am the next morning he was rescued by helicopter.

General Dugan has the distinction of being the last man to make a combat bailout from a Skyraider without 'help'. Partly because of its huge rudder, the Skyraider was not an easy airplane to bail out of. In the mid-1960s, the USAF and Stanley Aviation Company developed the Yankee extraction system, whereby a rocket was used to pull the pilot's seat out of the aircraft, enabling him to clear the vertical tail before his parachute deployed.

The first man to be extracted by the system was Major James E Holler, who parachuted safely after running into major problems whilst taking off from Pleiku. Soon afterward, on 11 June 1967, Majors Bob Russell and Jim Rausch of the 602nd SOS were hit by ground fire while rolling in on a target in an A-1E, number 132408. They had no choice but to bail out, being literally tugged from the Skyraider by their Yankee seats. The pair were rescued by that most familiar of helicopters, the HH-3E Jolly Green Giant.

*Four-ship formation
of A-1E Skyraiders
heads into harm's
way early in the war
(USAF)*

'Naked Fanny'

Only in 1969 were all Skyraider units centred in one location with the disbanding of the 6th SOS (with ET tailcode) at Pleiku and the stationing of the 1st, 22nd and 602nd SOS (TC, TS and TT tailcodes) at Nakhon Phanom, Thailand. In the vernacular of those who were there, the base was called 'Naked Fanny' or, simply, NKP, while its inhabitants were Hobos, Fireflies, Zorros, Nails, Candles and Nimrods. These were nicknames as well as call signs of (respectively) the Skyraider equipped 1st, 22nd and 602nd squadrons and for the squadrons operating OV-10 Broncos, C-123 flare ships and B-26 Invaders. NKP was an all-prop base in a supposedly jet war and in addition to fighting in North and South Vietnam more than a hundred of its personnel had died in a neighbouring country next door when President Nixon said that, 'No American has died fighting in Laos.'

The missions into Laos, like those elsewhere, were sometimes Sandy rescue escort sorties and sometimes close air support. The country itself was a different place to fly and fight, a land of looming karst towers

A-1E Skyraiders loaded with ordnance line up for take-off at Tan Son Nhut airbase near Saigon in 1965 (USAF)

and clinging fog, dense green forests and jagged ridges. Too, Laos was heavily populated with North Vietnamese guns. 'It's like going into the dragon's den,' one pilot remarked. Pilots found themselves fighting at night, under flares. They never liked the sputtering flares, which caused spatial disorientation and made it difficult to stay aligned on a target.

There were other problems. Verne Saxon was one of the first of a group of fresh second lieutenants to be put into the Skyraider as their first airplane (previously, experience in other combat aircraft types had been a requirement and the youngest Skyraider pilots had been captains and majors). Despite the Skyraider's many advantages, as late as 1969 Saxon found that no 'fix' had been found for the tendency of the four 20-mm cannons to jam and even to explode. One of Saxon's wingmen was almost killed when his plane's cannons began to cook off ammunition in flight and several rounds bracketed the pilot in his

cockpit. Saxon also noticed that the Skyraider did not agree with NKP's ramp of PSP (pierced steel planking) which was often dangerously slick from dripping oil or from rain. Tyre problems and problems with the pneumatic tail wheel, Saxon found, were characteristic of the A-1.

In a typical night mission (as described by Saxon), a pair of Skyraiders would take off together, proceed individually towards their target, and meet over the target where they would be directed by a FAC (forward air controller). Flares known as 'logs' dropped from a Candle C-123 would illuminate the target, perhaps an NVA (North Vietnamese Army) truck park. A typical load might be six 500-lb (227-kg) napalm canisters and two pods each carrying twenty-four 2.75-in rocket projectiles although, as Saxon says, 'Rockets were terrible at night. They would blind you and mark your aircraft [for the enemy].'

Napalm came in two varieties—finned and unfinned. The latter was accurate only in a 90-degree dive. On a typical mission, the two Skyraiders would acquire altitude separation and one would 'work' the

target while the other searched for guns. Saxon quickly learned to distinguish the categories of ground fire coming at him. '37-mm came in red balls. They were in clips of seven and they were slow. 23-mm had a more yellow-white colour and was higher velocity. The .51-calibre (12.8-mm) ZPU fire was even higher velocity. When a ZPU round hit your aircraft it would expand so you'd have an entry wound a half-inch wide and an exit hole big enough to poke your shoulders through.'

On 1 September 1968, Lt Col William A Jones, commander of the 602 SOS, was SANDY LEAD and on-scene commander of an attempt to rescue two crewmen of a downed F-4 Phantom. Reaching North Vietnam which, as usual, lay beneath tufts of white cloud and a blanket of dirty grey haze, Jones learned via radio that one of the Phantom crew had been captured and the other was evading. After a tragic misunderstanding in which other Phantom crews marked the wrong location for a rescue attempt, Jones led wingman Capt Paul A Meeks toward the correct spot. Directing the rescue force, Jones was hit by ground fire. His aircraft smoking, he pressed an

assault against NVA gun positions around the survivor—flying so low that one gun actually fired *down* at him from a slope.

Jones brought his A-1H Skyraider around in a tight turn, wings vertical to the ground, and attacked a gun site with 20-mm fire and CBU-38 cluster bombs. He heard the distinctive sound of more bullets puncturing his airplane's thin metal skin.

Heroic Effort

Incredibly, the hits ignited the rocket motor in Jones' Yankee extraction seat. Smoke churned around him and small crackling flames began to devour the legs of his flight suit. Jones levelled and blew his canopy, intending to bail out, but when he pulled the handle for the Yankee seat nothing happened.

Jones tried the secondary release. Again, nothing. Air rushing into his open cockpit fanned the flames. Paul Meeks in SANDY 2 shouted, 'Get out, Bill!

A-1G Skyraider 135021 (with different rear canopy shape than A-1E) banks over South Vietnam in 1965, coming back from a mission with bomb racks empty (USAF via R J Mills, Jr)

You're on fire! Get out now!'

NVA troops pressed closer to the survivor on the ground and, as if ignoring his own plight, Jones continued to radio information about the survivor's whereabouts to others in the rescue force. Jones' A-1H was now virtually engulfed in flames and was trailing a thick stream of smoke that swept back into the confined, overcast valley. Jones' transmitter died just as a new SANDY flight arrived to take over the rescue. Jones peeled back towards NKP and was able to make a straight-in approach and bring the Skyraider down, though it was a 100 per cent write-off. Badly burned, Jones talked from an ambulance stretcher, passing information which later led to a successful rescue of the survivor. Jones became one of

37 while the Skyraider-equipped 522nd had converted to Northrop F-5s. It is worthwhile to point out that Vietnamese pilots had no rest and recuperation leave, no end of their tour of duty: some logged a thousand or more combat missions; many simply flew until they died.

In fact, the people who manned the VNAF—and pilots in particular—seemed to an unusual degree to represent both the best and the worst. One Skyraider pilot who did quite well before changing jobs was a certain Lieutenant Loan who is remembered today not for his skills in the A-1H but for his later existence as a Saigon police chief. With justification, Loan used a pistol to shoot a captured Viet Cong terrorist in the head and the Press photograph of that event became perhaps the single best-known picture of the entire war, so that Loan's pilot days were virtually forgotten. From the beginning of the war until the very end, a few Vietnamese pilots were unmotivated and uninterested. A tremendous number of VNAF fliers, however, displayed courage that was almost beyond belief.

In 1970, as part of the 'Vietnamization' programme which grew from the Guam Doctrine, a number of VNAF Skyraiders were retrofitted with 'zero time' R-3350 engines. The 2700-hp R-3350, remembered so vividly by Skyraider pilots for coughing smoke and dripping oil, had the qualities of being powerful, durable, and resistant to battle damage. But it was damndably difficult to maintain, repair or use and by 1970 the best R-3350 mechanics in the world—US Navy petty officers—had retired or moved on to other things. As Nguyen Cao Nguyen, chief of maintenance for the South Vietnamese air arm, has pointed out, the VNAF never attained the high maintenance standard of other services. American officers scoffed that the Wright engine was the wrong engine, at least for VNAF users.

Though he became Premier and later Vice President of his country, the charismatic Air Marshal Nguyen Cao Ky maintained his close ties to the A-1 Skyraider community and especially to the VNAF 83rd Tactical Wing at Saigon's Tan Son Nhut airbase, which had a charter for special operations against North Vietnam. The 83rd reportedly used Skyraiders to cover the insertion into North Vietnam of elite teams from the euphemistically-named Studies and Observation Group (SOG). Both VNAF and USAF Skyraiders also covered US Army Special Forces teams which were dropped into Laos for road reconnaissance along the Ho Chi Minh Trail. From 1967, Air Marshal Ky had turned over the role of VNAF Chief of Staff to Tran Van Minh, who held the post until the end in 1975—but Ky himself continued to fly Skyraiders on a regular basis.

NKP-based Skyraiders helped cover the Son Tay Raid, the November 1970 action aimed at rescuing American prisoners of war in North Vietnam. This was a unique event which stood out during the long 'bombing halt' (November 1968–March 1972) bet-

only twelve Air Force men in Vietnam (and two Skyraider pilots) to earn the Medal of Honor, which is given for 'conspicuous gallantry and intrepidity in action at the risk of [one's] life above and beyond the call of duty.'

While the US Navy retired the Skyraider from carrier decks (replacing it with the Grumman A-6 Intruder), the VNAF developed and expanded. President Nixon's policy, enunciated in an August 1969 speech which became known as the Guam Doctrine, was to call upon Asian allies to supply the manpower for their defence. In short, the US was pulling its men out. To compensate, the VNAF grew until it became the fourth largest air arm in the world. A few side-by-side A-1Es (and similar A-1Gs) were added to the inventory of single-seat A-1H and A-1J aeroplanes, and by late 1969 the VNAF had the following Skyraider fighter squadrons: 514th at Bien Hoa; 516th at Da Nang; 518th at Bien Hoa; 530th at Pleiku. The 520th at Binh Thuy had operated Skyraiders briefly before converting to the Cessna A-

LEFT
Lugging many pounds of typical Skyraider attire, Major Bernard Fisher climbs aboard a camouflaged A-1E Skyraider at Pleiku on 5 May 1966. Two months earlier, in a courageous rescue of another pilot during the battle of A Shau, Fisher had become the first airman of the Vietnam war to earn the Medal of Honor (USAF)

ABOVE
Enscounced in A-1E Skyraider cockpit, Major Bernard Fisher prepares for a mission (USAF)

ween two major campaigns 'up North'. (Though the US did not bomb North Vietnam during the long 'bombing halt', Skyraiders were extremely busy in Laos and South Vietnam, and—as the war spread to a fourth country—Cambodia). By early 1972—on the eve of the resumption of bombing North Vietnam— the three squadrons at NKP had been reduced to one, the 1st SOS (TC tailcode) being the final American Skyraider unit in the conflict.

Already adept at coping with MiGs, missiles and AAA, the Skyraider confronted a new adversary with the March 1972 'Easter invasion' by Hanoi's regular forces (the event which also triggered renewed bombing of the North). For the first time, NVA troops fielded the SA-7 man-portable SAM (surface-to-air missile). Skyraider pilots also found, for the first time, that they were fighting tanks—the PT-76 and T-54 tanks introduced by the enemy in this new stage of fighting. The Skyraider was to prove highly vulnerable to the shoulder-mounted SA-7, and no fewer than three A-1s were shot down in two days in May 1972.

Sandy Missions

Even with an increased threat against them Sky-raiders continued to fly the Sandy mission covering combat rescue up North. Pilots and aircrew got into the habit of referring to a particular rescue mission by the call sign of the downed airman they wanted to save ('You were there when we got BAT 21 out?' 'I was flying SANDY LEAD on the day we went after BENGAL 505'. 'Remember when we went in to try to get SHOWTIME 109?') An especially remarkable rescue was pulled off in May 1972 when Skyraiders picked up Captain Roger C Locher, who had ejected from a Phantom on 10 May 1972 and was on the ground in North Vietnam for *twenty-three days*.

The Sandy mission, which had resulted in so many combat rescues, had to be taken over by a new aircraft type in order to free USAF Skyraiders for delivery to the VNAF under the 'Vietnamization' programme. The Vought A-7D aircraft (which never acquired its nickname Corsair in USAF service) was chosen for the role. A-1 Skyraiders flew the final Sandy sortie on 7 November 1972 when they covered the site at Quang Ngai where a US Army UH-1 Huey helicopter had been downed with seven people aboard. Defying heavy winds and clinging murk as a typhoon began around them, the Skyraiders located the seven survivors, used 20-mm fire to hold off NVA troops, and brought about a successful rescue. This final Sandy mission was also the final Skyraider mission by the 1st SOS, which went out of business

Four A-1E Skyraiders of the USAF's 34th Tactical Group in flight over South Vietnam near Bien Hoa on 25 June 1965 (USAF)

leaving the VNAF the only Skyraider operator in the conflict. By the 27 January 1973 cease-fire which brought about the American withdrawal, the VNAF actually had more Skyraiders than it could handle and was putting some in storage.

The end came 30 months later. On 30 April 1975 with NVA tanks on the outskirts of Saigon and the final evacuation taking place, a VNAF AC-119K Stinger gunship flanked by two A-1H Skyraiders lifted out of Tan Son Nhut airport for a final show of futility and courage, engaging the oncoming enemy amid a criss-crossing stream of gunfire and SA-7 rockets. SA-7s finally claimed the Stinger and one A-1H, leaving the other Skyraider—the very last aircraft in combat in Southeast Asia—heading up the Saigon River, still fighting.

As for Bernie Fisher's aircraft, 132649, it was crashed *again* at Qui Nhon in 1967 by a pilot who bellied in without disposing of his centreline tank.

FAR RIGHT
While Air Commandos flew the Skyraider in Southeast Asia, training was carried out at their home station, Hurlburt Field, Florida. Typical of Skyraiders used to train USAF pilots for the Vietnam conflict was A-1E 132436 (Norman Taylor)

Already featured on page 136, this is another view of 'old 405' being retired from service on 10 April 1968. Aircraft 135300 of the 'Fist of the Fleet', VA-25 went to the museum at Pensacola, Florida. Though this was billed as the retirement ceremony for the Skyraider aircraft type, at this time the EA-1F version was still in service (USN via R J Mills, Jr)

The aircraft was salvaged again and returned to Hurlburt Field where it was used to train pilots. Belatedly, 132649 made its way to the US Air Force Museum in Dayton, Ohio where it is on display today—the first Medal of Honor aircraft in history to be preserved in a museum.

Post-war Spads

A number of other Skyraiders are on display in museums, one fine example being AD-4B bureau number 132261 with the US Marine Corps collection at Quantico, Virginia, maintained in an early 1950s sea blue paint scheme. The Smithsonian Institution's National Air and Space Museum has acquired a former VNAF A-1H, bureau number not firmly determined, now located at the Gerber preservation facility in Silver Hill, Maryland.

More than a few Skyraiders have appeared on the airshow circuit as restored 'warbirds', many of these being earlier AD-4 (A-1D) aeroplanes painted in the insignia of Vietnam-era A-1H Spads. Most are in US Navy colours and quite a sight they make, beating up the airshow crowds at Oshkosh and other warbird convocations. One 'warbird' was beautifully restored in Air Force markings of the 1st Special Operations Squadron replete with TC tailcode, this being AD-4 (A-1D) Skyraider 126970 posing as an A-1H/J. This aircraft, sadly, was lost in a Virginia air crash which took the life of the owner and his wife.

Chapter 8

The Skyraider and the BAT-21B Rescue

'Captain Fred C Boli distinguished himself by gallantry in connection with military operations against an opposing armed force in Southeast Asia from 3 April 1972 to 6 April 1972. During this period, Captain Boli flew in support of a Search and Rescue mission to recover downed American crewmembers located ten miles south of the Demilitarized Zone in South Vietnam in the middle of an advancing army of heavily armed hostile troops. Although forced to fly at low altitudes because of the overcast weather, Captain Boli disregarded personal safety and repeatedly exposed his slow-moving A-1 Skyraider to intense anti-aircraft and small-arms fire to protect the survivors, thus insuring their eventual successful recovery. By his gallantry and devotion to duty, Captain Boli has reflected great credit upon himself and The United States Air Force.

—citation to accompany award of the Silver Star medal

No test of the Skyraider was more demanding than its trial by fire in Vietnam. And nothing in Vietnam was more of a challenge than the Sandy mission—the job of providing on-scene command (OSC) for combat rescues of downed airmen in places where enemy fire was intense, danger was everywhere, and a pilot's adrenaline level could go over the top.

The A-1 Skyraider pilots who flew Sandy missions were genuine heroes—dedicated, selfless, and willing to lay their lives right on the line. Most would not have been able to say why. It wasn't usually about God, honour or country. It had something to do with taking care of your own.

Of the many courageous rescues led by Skyraider pilots, none involved greater drama than what came to be known as the BAT 21 Sar (search and rescue). This largest and costliest rescue operation of the war occurred in the midst of North Vietnam's ferocious Easter Invasion (beginning Good Friday, 31 March 1972). The rescue later became the subject of a fictionalized account (Anderson, William C, *Bat-21*. New York: Bantam, 1980). A motion picture based on the book was released in 1988.

The volume focuses on the experiences of survivor Lt Col Iceal (Gene) Hambleton and says relatively little about the courageous A-1 Skyraider pilots who ultimately brought about Hambleton's rescue after 14 days on the ground. In the book, the author acknowledges that he has manufactured characters, conversations and events. An *accurate* version of the story would emphasize not only Hambleton's ordeal but the role of Skyraider pilots, Jolly Green rescue crews, and many others.

BAT 21 was the radio call sign for Douglas EB-66C Destroyer 54-0466 of the 42nd Tactical Electronic Warfare Squadron, 355th Tactical Fighter Wing (tailcode JW), flying from Korat airbase, Thailand. (Hambleton himself was BAT-21B). On 4 April 1972, just four days into Hanoi's massive spring offensive, the camouflaged EB-66C Destroyer lifted into the sky from Korat, turned toward the Hanoi region, and began its mission of jamming enemy communications and radars. Together with a second EB-66C, callsign BAT 22, the electronic warfare aircraft was supporting a cell of B-52D Stratofortresses, bombing near the 17th Parallel.

This was a little-known but incredibly risky mission. Without getting much attention, it had cost the losses of five RB-66 and EB-66 aeroplanes earlier in the conflict.

Lt Col Gene Hambleton, at the rather advanced age of fifty-three, was an extremely capable EB-66C navigator and electronics officer. He had been in and out of the conflict and probably knew as much as

Balls A Fire, Lt Dale R Townsend's A-1H Skyraider of the 1st SOS at Nakhon Phanom in April 1970 is believed to be airplane 134622, the craft which Capt Fred C Boli crash-landed at Long Thien, Laos. All USAF Skyraiders were eventually turned over to the Vietnamese Air Force (USAF)

TOP LEFT
*Captain Richard G Head (now a retired brigadier general)
suffered battle damage in this 1965 mission in A-1E
Skyraider 132668 and bellied-in on a foamed runway at
Bien Hoa. Aircraft belonged to the 602nd Fighter
Squadron (Commando) (USAF)*

LEFT
*The value of the A-1 Skyraider as a platform for rescue
missions was beyond dispute. Much earlier in the war, this
view of an A-1E with typical ordnance dramatized what
the 'Spad' could tote into battle beneath its wings. As the
Hambleton search and rescue operation unfolded,
Skyraiders again had to go into battle carrying plenty of
'convincing' (USAF)*

ABOVE
*The BAT 21 search and rescue mission, coinciding as it did
with North Vietnam's spring offensive, was aimed at
rescuing Lt Col Iceal (Gene) Hambleton, crew member of
an EB-66C aircraft similar to this one. Seen here at
Takhli, Thailand in 1969, the EB-66C was highly
effective in jamming Hanoi's radars (USAF)*

anyone about how to jam, confuse and deceive Hanoi's electronic defences. In fact, F-4E Phantom back-seater Lt Col Steven Bricker later expressed his regret at inadvertently strobing Hambleton's EB-66C after being cautioned not to. 'The jamming gear on that bird fried my Phantom's radar and its antenna. We got back to our base and the electronic "fixer" guys had to give the Phantom a complete overhaul.'

Inside his EB-66C, Hambleton wore the usual G-suit, harness, oxygen mask and other items of equipment over the nomex flight coveralls which were going to become his uniform for the next couple of weeks. The usual odds and ends needed during a flight, including a crisp pack of Marlboro cigarettes, were strewn in front of him. In the days ahead, Lt Col Hambleton was to profoundly regret not carrying those Marlboros in his flight suit pocket!

As the EB-66C began to work in the Hanoi region, what may have been a 'lucky hit' from a Soviet-built SA-2 *Guideline* missile changed Gene Hambleton's life forever. One moment, he was bent over his scope. An instant later, his EB-66C had been blown to bits and he was tumbling in space—the sole survivor of a five-man crew!

It took almost twenty minutes for Hambleton's parachute to bring him down in the midst of the inaptly-named Demilitarized Zone (DMZ). Hambleton was stunned, injured, and without nicotine.

Sandy Mission

It is time for Skyraider pilot Fred Boli to enter this narrative.

Nowadays if you want to find Colonel Fred C Boli, you'll have to visit the scholarly-looking campus of the National Defense University (NDU), located on flat green land along the Potomac River in Washington, DC. The Russian-speaking Colonel Boli, a key US Air Force expert on the Soviet Union, works at a 'think tank' co-located with NDU, the Strategic Concepts Development Center. Nowadays, Fred is likely to be analysing a Soviet pronouncement or drafting a report over his computer—but he still looks like the young fighter pilot he once was, when young men went to war in a very old aeroplane.

Fred C Boli is a zoomie. That's a graduate of the USAF Academy at Colorado Springs. In February 1971, he arrived at Nakhon Phanom to join the 1st Special Operations Squadron, the former First Air Commando which was also known as the 'Hobos', the

Life was never easy for Skyraider pilots, and a crackup near the end of the runway was likely to happen more often than many wanted to admit. With a Kaman HH-43F helicopter overhead, this A-1E Skyraider seems to be trying to set itself on fire but without complete success (Courtesy Norman Taylor)

very last American unit to employ the A-1 Skyraider in Southeast Asia.

Fred Boli had trained extensively in the aircraft and was at home in the ancient, prop-driven, single-seat A-1H and A-1J, as well as the multi-place A-1E variant. A captain at the time, Boli was assigned A-1J aircraft 142021, which he promptly nicknamed *Devilish Diane* after his wife. This aeroplane had been flown earlier by Jim Egbert of the 6th SOS at Pleiku who'd had the name *Sun Tan Sam* painted on the nose.

The USAF had acquired the Skyraider only very belatedly, but the men who flew the aircraft developed a special fondness for it and always considered themselves a cut above the jet jocks who flew 'fast movers'. Fred Boli and other latecomer Skyraider pilots were very much aware that two of their predecessors—Bernard F Fisher and William H

Jones 3rd—had earned the Medal of Honor for combat rescues performed while flying the Skyraider.

The Skyraider is best known for the 'Sandy' role, supporting forces employed to rescue fliers downed behind enemy lines. But, as has been noted elsewhere in this narrative, Skyraider pilots were also flying and fighting in Laos, where NVA (North Vietnamese

BELOW
The only stateside location for US Air Force Skyraiders was Hurlburt Field in the Florida panhandle, home of the Special Operations units. The highly appropriate AD tailcode for this A-1E belongs to the 4407th Combat Crew Training Squadron (later 8th Special Operations Squadron) at Hurlburt (Courtesy Norman Taylor)

BOTTOM RIGHT
Two A-1E Skyraiders escort a CH-3C helicopter on a rescue mission in Southeast Asia (USAF)

Army) forces were heavily entrenched. Part of their mission was to support friendly Hmong tribes people, led by General Vang Pao, who had been fighting the NVA for years. Vang Pao's forces were headquartered at Long Thien in northern Laos, at an airfield called LS-20A which was also the location of civilian-clothed USAF forward air controllers (FACs) flying unmarked Cessna O-1 Bird Dogs.

Crash Landing

After years of being somewhat distant from ground fighting, Long Thien came under heavy NVA attack mid-way through Fred Boli's combat tour and on 16 September 1971, Fred had the distinction of being the first person to belly-land a Skyraider at LS-20A. The aircraft was not *Diane* but, rather, A-1H

Skyraider 134622 which is listed on official records as being 'written off' the day of the belly landing. In fact, that's not exactly what happened.

Using the call sign HOBO 44, Captain Boli was pressing an attack against NVA near Long Thien. The Skyraider had proven ideal for close-quarters air-to-ground work. Most of the time, it could withstand enemy fire. This time, however, NVA gunners got lucky.

Several times, Fred Boli went storming down on NVA positions to unload ordnance. In the daytime, it was never certain how much they were shooting at you, but he saw plenty of muzzle flashes and was aware of gunfire whipping around his A-1H. He was getting low on both ordnance and fuel when the 'hit' with his number on it arrived.

A hit from ground fire caused Boli to lose oil pressure. There was no prospect of getting home. His

TOP
Rarely-seen ET tailcode belonged to the 6th Special Operations Squadron at Pleiku. A-1H Skyraider 142059 taxies out of the Pleiku revetment with a typical load of fuel, rockets, and unfinned napalm (Robert F Dorr)

LEFT
Bristling with ordnance, a US Air Force A-1E 'wide-body' Skyraiders of the 1st SOS taxi out for take-off at Nakhon Phanom (NKP) RTAFB on 2 April 1972 (USAF)

ABOVE
A 'Cherry Picker' prepares to pluck a battle-damaged Skyraider from the Bien Hoa runway following a successful wheels up landing. The Skyraider's toughness was legendary, and this example would almost certainly have returned to active service after necessary repairs (USAF)

LEFT
US Air Force A-1H Skyraider of the 8th SOS poses during a training mission from Eglin AFB, Florida, in 1970 (Harry Gann)

A-1H was badly damaged and LS-20A was the only runway within reach.

The LS-20A airstrip had routinely handled Bird Dogs and T-28s, as well as an occasional C-123 or Pilatus Porter, but no one had ever landed a Skyraider there, especially a 'hot' Skyraider without hydraulics. Fred was extremely cautious as he fought to bring his A-1H down safely. Writing about his experience in the third person, he later said:

'During the emergency forced landing at LS-20A, the tyres blew out while Capt Boli was attempting to stop 622 on the 3000-ft rough surface. The resultant loss of directional control necessitated gear retraction to prevent 622 from impacting the karst [limestone cliff] at the north end of the runway. At the time of landing LS-20A was under NVA attack, so bailout was not a viable option for Capt Boli.

'He was later awarded the Air Medal for saving the aircraft by landing on a field that no one could recall having ever before having a Skyraider land on. The gear was torn off when 622 was pulled by its tail to

*South Vietnamese Air Force (VNAF) A-1Hs of the 23rd
Tactical Wing, 3rd Air Division, being 'bombed up' by
armourers at Bien Hoa AB. Detailed information
regarding VNAF Skyraider operations is included in
Robert C Mikesh's highly acclaimed* FLYING
DRAGONS: The South Vietnamese Air Force *(ISBN
0-85045-819-6), an Osprey book published in 1988*
(Norman Taylor)

clear the runway. Subsequently, A-1H 622 was destroyed when a [Sikorsky CH-54A Sky Crane] helicopter dropped it off the south end of LS-20A because, while 622 was being transported beneath the helicopter, high winds caused the A-1H to swing outside safety limits . . .'

The unfortunate loss of 134622 was especially distressing to squadron maintenance officer Captain Alfred M Cook, who in an effort to save the Skyraider had travelled to Long Thien in an unmarked Air America C-123, the interior of which still reeked of with cow manure.

BAT 21 Sar

Boli's award of the Silver Star (the third highest American award for bravery) came during the massive search and rescue mission (SAR, or Sar) which took place in the days immediately following north Vietnam's massive 31 March 1972 invasion—the so-called Easter offensive—this being the same provocation which led President Nixon to mine Haiphong harbour and resume regular bombing in the North.

Right in the middle of the heavy fighting, EB-66C navigator Gene Hambleton ejected and parachuted into the midst of a battle involving at least three infantry divisions.

As is noted in an official history, Captain Jimmie D Kempton, pilot of an OV-10 Bronco operating from Da Nang, talked to Hambleton as he descended in his parachute. It took a leisurely (and nicotine-free) twenty minutes or so for the chute to bring Hambleton to earth. During this time, Kempton reported that the region was completely blanketed by clouds and that fixing the exact position of the survivor was difficult. Captain Kempton descended through clouds and located Hambleton visually, his chute still visible from the air.

Within moments, two A-1 Skyraiders diverted from another mission were overhead, working with Hambleton over his survival radio. Hambleton spotted NVA troops (some of whom were seeking to capture *him*) and directed the Skyraider pilots who came in under low clouds hanging over the river valley. Hambleton called off positions of fire, watched the Skyraider ordnance impact, and gave the A-1 pilots corrections based on his observations.

BELOW RIGHT
Fully-armed VNAF A-1H of the 23rd Tactical Wing awaits its pilot. Revetments were essential in order to protect VNAF air assets from VC mortar attacks. (Norman Taylor)

BELOW
Bomb racks empty, a VNAF A-1H of the 23rd Tactical Wing taxies in at Bien Hoa AB after a sortie (Norman Taylor)

Meanwhile, Kempton had flown southward, making calls to find someone to go in and pick up Hambleton. Soon he was returning with four US Army helicopters in tow—two AH-1G Cobra gunships and two UH-1H Huey passenger-carrying 'slicks'.

So quickly it defied belief, two of the four choppers were shot down whilst approaching Hambleton's position. One UH-1H Huey was completely destroyed with no survivors. The Cobra, call sign BLUE GHOST 28, was able to reach the beach and its two crewmen were rescued.

Contrary to the assertions in the work of fiction based on Hambleton's rescue, the primary purpose of the men and warplanes committed to battle in the area was to engage the NVA rather than to rescue Hambleton. The fact remains, Gene Hambleton was a genuine hero—hunkering on the ground and communicating with friendly aircraft while the land battle was underway. Skyraiders using the callsigns SANDY and HOBO were over Hambleton's head constantly, fought a prolonged engagement with NVA forces, and directed an attempt at rescue which failed tragically.

Hambleton's first day on the ground reached 2100 hours and a new OV-10 Bronco, call sign NAIL 59, reached the scene. This OV-10, like others to follow, came from the 23rd Tactical Air Support Squadron at Nakhon Phanom and was a new version with the Pave Nail precision Loran day/night navigation pod hung beneath the fuselage. This device provided the Bronco with precision Loran navigation equipment,

a light intensification viewer, a laser designator, and a computer system. Although the Bronco had heretofore been flown by one pilot on combat missions, the Pave Nail Bronco carried two, pilot and weapon systems operator.

The 23rd TASS had used the NAIL call sign for years, so this vital new piece of equipment was apparently named after the call sign rather than the other way around. The Pave Nail system had proved itself on rescue missions by accurately pinpointing survivors again and again. With darkness over them, NAIL 59 established radio contact with Hambleton and located him a thousand metres north of the town of Cam Lo on the north bank of the Mien Giang River.

Air–Ground Actions

Fred Boli's logbook shows that on 2 April 1972, he took A-1J Skyraider aircraft 142021 (*Devilish Diane*) from Nakhon Phanom and, using the call sign SANDY 1, deployed to Da Nang for the BAT 21B Sar, flying 4.1 hours. Boli apparently could not have known until the following morning about the EB-66C crewman being on the ground. Meanwhile, four men comprising the crews of two Pave Nail Broncos from Nakhon Phanom—one crew being Captain Rocky O Smith and Captain Richard M Atchison—prepared to arrive over Hambleton, now better known by most airmen in the region as BAT 21B—at first light.

Hambleton had meanwhile taken refuge in a big clump of bushes surrounded by a very large field, and reported that there were North Vietnamese troops still all around. The Broncos, Skyraiders and other covering aircraft thus needed to put down a ring of area-denial ordnance around the BAT 21B survivor. In the foul weather, the Pave Nail Bronco crew of Smith and Atchison played a major role in directing strikes that prevented the NVA from seizing Hambleton.

Smith and Atchison landed at Da Nang instead of their home station and met with COVEY forward air controllers (O-2 pilots) and Army advisors to explain Hambleton's situation and the facts of the battle unfolding north of the Cam Lo River.

Meanwhile, at Nakhon Phanom, another Pave Nail Bronco crew headed up by Captain Bill Henderson went aloft to relieve NAIL 59 at the scene. It might be noted, here, that in Vietnam the namesakes of several well-known American generals distinguished themselves. The Army's Major General George S Patton (a son) and the Air Force's Skyraider pilot Lieutenant James H Doolittle 3rd (a grandson) were examples. Serving as the second crewman in the rear seat of Henderson's Bronco, call sign NAIL 38, was Captain Mark Clark, also a grandson of a four-star World War 2 commander.

Bronco Shootdown

In the cockpit of Skyraider *Devilish Diane* or 142021, again as flight leader or SANDY 1 (but with squadron commander Lt Col Martin Barbena on his wing), Captain Fred Boli was covering Hambleton on the ground on 3 April, when another loss was suffered. With Bill Henderson at the controls and Mark Clark operating the system, OV-10 Pave Nail Bronco 68-3789, call sign NAIL 38, from the 23rd TASS joined the combination search and air-ground battle.

In conjunction with the offensive, the North Vietnamese had moved their missile batteries farther south than ever before. While engaging the NVA and attempting to communicate with Hambleton, a SAM missile came flying up in the open sky beneath the overcast, missed the lower wing of Barbena's Skyraider by no more than ten feet (three metres)—apparently not tracking on Boli or Barbena at all—and slammed into the OV-10.

Another pilot describes what happend to the Pave Nail Bronco:

Just as they started to turn, they caught it right in the tail booms. Blew that OV-10 to pieces. Just a tumbling ball of fire, sailing down to the river. Two chutes came out of the fireball—beautiful. Mark [Clark] landed south of the river, south and east of Hambleton. Henderson landed north in a big field—within 500 metres of BAT 21B. Henderson told me after his release that ten or fifteen people came out of the

*General view of the A-1
ramp at Bien Hoa AB*
(Norman Taylor)

woods and chased him. He found a clump of bamboo and jumped in—they couldn't find him. That night, a group came out and started cutting down the bamboo. They used it for camouflage. They worked right over to Bill [Henderson]'s shelter. He doubled up with machetes going over his head. They cut all of his bamboo down, [saw him, and captured him]. He was taken north.

Mark [Clark] found a barbed wire enclosed area—figured it was a good place to hide. He crawled under the wire. We [other Pave Nail Broncos, directing strikes by Skyraiders] worked the whole area over with Loran weapon deliveries—then the clouds broke and we worked the fighters visually.

To backtrack slightly for another view of the NAIL 38 shootdown, Captain Fred Boli orbited overhead in his Skyraider, Barbena beside him, and observed parachutes from both OV-10 crew members. Now, three survivors were on the ground, all within two kilometres of each other near the Dong Ha River with fighting going on all around them. The Bronco pilot, Bill Henderson, call sign NAIL 38A, was—as indicated—overwhelmed by NVA. Many of the participants in that action, to his day, are under the mistaken impression that the North Vietnamese overwhelmed and killed Henderson. In fact, he became a POW (prisoner of war).

Mark Clark, alias NAIL 38B, began a valiant effort to evade the North Vietnamese, not far away from Gene Hambleton, alias BAT 21B, but too far away to link up with him.

Fred Boli logged 4.7 combat hours in his Skyraider that day (bringing his total Southeast Asia combat time to 280.1 hours; it eventually became 335.1) but despite repeated efforts by him and many others, no way could be found to rescue BAT 21B or NAIL 38B.

4 April was no better. Numerous sorties were flown against the invading North Vietnamese and in support of the two downed airmen. Fred Boli is quick to make the point that he was only one of many pilots in the air, and indeed he logged another 3.0 combat hours as SANDY 5 in airplane 142021. The perils of the downed EB-66C and OV-10 crew members deepened, however, as the weather grew worse and a blanket of clinging grey murk enclosed itself over the battlefield.

Major James R Harding, operations officer and future commander of the 1st SOS, was flight leader or SANDY 1 in the A-1 Skyraider force from Nakhon Phanom on 4 April. It appears that Harding was able to get within eyesight of Hambleton on several occasions. (Harding's published biography is not kind to the Skyraider. It says that he 'was in Southeast Asia during 1965 where he flew F-100s and again in 1970–71 flying aircraft'. The type is not named. Other pilots say that Harding was a staunch advocate of the Skyraider and—as one puts it—'the bravest sonofabitch I've ever seen.') Harding used a variety of ordnance against the North Vietnamese and inflicted severe casualties, but the land battle

continued and the two survivors remained on the ground.

Jolly Green

Throughout the offensive and the rescue effort, the weather in North and South Vietnam was, in Boli's word, 'crummy'. This was far from unusual. Skyraider pilots had long since adjusted themselves to the idea of flying when fog or haze clung to the ground and low clouds impeded visibility. But now the weather continued to deteriorate.

Nobody flew on 5 April. Nobody could. Ceiling and visibility were zero-zero. On the ground, NAIL 38B (Clark) and BAT 21B (Hambleton)—not able to link up with each other—continued to hunker down and hide from the North Vietnamese. The weather failed to improve. Clark's experiences on this day are not a matter of record. Hambleton was dying for a cigarette.

Again, it must be emphasized that A-1 Skyraider pilots and others were involved in far more than

efforts to rescue the two downed airmen. Apparently early on 6 April—with the weather still lousy— spotter aircraft from two different units, a COVEY and a NAIL, were supporting the rescue effort when they came upon a column of North Vietnamese tanks. In this offensive, the enemy had introduced PT-76 and T-54 tanks not previously seen in the fighting.

Being used in large numbers for the first time in the war during this spring offensive, the tanks were

rumbling down Highway One, the thoroughfare which author Bernard Fall had named the 'Street Without Joy'. Using secure voice communications, these fliers brought in a strike by six B-52D Stratofortresses. Bombing as usual from very high altitude with guidance and direction from the spotters, the Arc Light mission (B-52 strike) destroyed 35 tanks as well as the command bunker of the NVA division in the area.

Those in the air above the downed survivors continued to seek two objectives—first, to stop the NVA invasion forces, disrupt their movement and cut their supply lines, and second, to beat down the defences around Hambleton and Clark so that a pickup could be made. One pilot described how, for a brief time at least, the area around the survivors looked quiet:

'We had bombed it, we had destroyed all the troop camps, all the bridges, and the headquarters building, all the firebases in the area. There was no movement.' Most of this 'neutralizing' of the NVA had been done by Skyraiders.

While Harding, Boli, Barbena and other Skyraider

pilots kept trying to bring off a rescue, the tragedy deepened.

When the weather finally broke on 6 April 1972 and B-52 strikes were called in on the NVA in the region, Boli and his fellow 'Hobos' believed that a rescue was now possible. As SANDY 1, or the on-scene commander (OSC), Boli attempted to bring in rescue helicopters, call signs JOLLY GREEN 60 and 67. In late afternoon, Boli directed that air strikes in the area be terminated. At his direction, SANDY 3 laid white phosphorus smoke to mark Hambleton's location for the rescuers.

The chopper, an HH-53C known as JOLLY GREEN 67 went into rescue Hambleton. The plan was to run in over Clark's position on a northwesterly heading, cross the river and the road, pick up Hambleton, make a left turn, pick up Clark about one kilometre south, and exit out to the south.

Boli heard the chopper telling Hambleton to ignite a flare ('BAT 21B, pop your smoke, pop your smoke!'). In the trees, 100 metres from Hambleton, JOLLY GREEN 67 proclaimed, 'I'm hit, I'm hit. They got a fuel line!' Frantic communications followed. Hambleton apparently realized the chopper would not be able to reach him and refrained from making smoke. Boli, Hambleton and others tried to warn the pilot of the badly-damaged helicopter not to fly over a nearby village, known to be heavily entrenched with NVA.

JOLLY 67's difficulties, according to one version of the event, were caused because a crew member had pushed down the radio transmit button. Skyraider pilots including Boli were screaming, 'Turn left, don't turn right, turn left.' But JOLLY 67 could not hear because the microphone button was down. The Skyraider pilots watched as JOLLY 67 limped back across the river. A flame shot out below the main rotor. The helicopter nosed up, rolled left 90 degrees, and started to disintegrate.

To quote a report written by Fred Boli not with the hindsight of history (one version of which, years later, gives the helicopter's call sign as JOLLY 62) but within days, on 18 April 1972:

'I was now crossing behind JOLLY GREEN 67 strafing the village just east of him. As I pulled out of the pass I noted that he had now overturned the egress heading slightly and was headed southwest. I ordered him, 'Turn left, JOLLY, turn south'. Someone interrupted with, 'Turn right'. JOLLY GREEN 67 hesitated and I again ordered, 'No! Turn left, JOLLY, turn south!' He hesitated and I was about to order him to climb when as I passed by on a strafe pass I observed a fire suddenly break out. Pieces flew off the tail rotor and struck the main rotor, causing it to break up.' At 1740 hours, JOLLY GREEN 67 went in, all men aboard killed in a failed combat rescue.

In the book *Bat-21*, the author readily discloses that for dramatic effect he manufactures people, conversations and events. (The author openly invents a fictitious OV-10 pilot who refuses orders to go home while the rescue efforts are underway, as well as an absurd scene in which the Chief of Staff in the Pentagon worries about Hambleton personally). The book (read, but not relied upon as a source for this narrative) suggests strongly that the crew of JOLLY GREEN 67 lost their lives because they didn't know what they were doing. The report by Fred Boli, which manufactures nothing and was written at the time tells it otherwise:

Heroic Crew

'I find myself at a loss of words [for] the selfless bravery [of] the crew of JOLLY GREEN 67. Only the Medal of Honor, our nation's highest decoration, can adequately begin to recognize the valour and gallantry demonstrated by the crew of JOLLY GREEN 67 in the face of an overwhelmingly superior enemy force . . .' The HH-53C crew received the Air Force Cross instead, posthumously.

Mark Clark observed the destruction of the HH-53C helicopter from south of the river. Clark, or NAIL 38B, witnessed a North Vietnamese signalman on the river bank. While Clark's thoughts at that particular moment in the conflict are not known, he might be forgiven for wishing he had a high-powered sniper's rifle. In one of those scenes which etch themselves forever into the minds of men at war, Clark watched the North Vietnamese signalman jerk out a red scarf and begin waving. All of the American hi-tech of the era, including Loran and lasers and 'smart' bombs, had come up against a scraggly Asian holding a swath of red. Whenever aircraft came in at low level, the North Vietnamese waved his scarf and every gun in the region began to open up.

For several more days, with the area around Hambleton and Clark described officially as 'pretty hot', airmen continued to support the downed survivors.

A-1 Skyraiders stationed at Nakhon Phanom, some of them operating from Da Nang, continued to fly close support above the men on the ground. Incredibly, throughout the first two weeks of the NVA spring offensive and the protracted rescue effort, not a single Skyraider was lost in combat. One airman has a vivid recollection of a single-seater (A-1H or A-1J) pulling off from a bomb run over a North Vietnamese infantry division, coughing up gouts of black smoke, and limping home safely.

A further attempt to pick up the two survivors with HH-53C Jolly Green helicopters had to be abandoned as too risky. At one point, planners still trying to work out a rescue of Clark and Hambleton discussed sending a US Army light observation helicopter into the combat zone at night to pick up the two men. This was in the era before night observation capabilities had been developed fully and, in the end, the idea did not seem practical. Only after discussions with a Marine officer at Da Nang, the would-be rescuers determined that a US Navy Seal team could work upriver to rescue the pair.

After receiving word of the new plan Clark and Hambleton started working their way downriver. Clark was closest to the river. He swam and floated down the river and was first to be greeted by fellow

TOP RIGHT
Less than fully-laden VNAF A-1H Skyraider of the 23rd TW taxies out prior to a sortie from Bien Hoa AB (Norman Taylor)

RIGHT
Gear down, flaps extended, a US Air Force A-1H named Buttler's Best of the 602nd SOS returns from a long range Sandy mission. The external fuel tank under the right wing is balanced by an electronic countermeasures pod (USAF)

Americans. Hambleton had to traverse a full mile of mine field—it took him four hours to reach the river. After resting, he crossed the river, found a log and began floating downstream. After dawn, he hid in the foliage along the bank.

For three nights, Hambleton made his way downriver, his progress closely followed by A-1 Skyraider and OV-10 Bronco pilots overhead. On the fourth day of movement (the fourteenth of his ordeal) Hambleton sighted a sampan. Using a pre-arranged signal, he called out his rank and his favourite colour. The men on the sampan acknowledged. They took Hambleton aboard and covered him with leaves. His ordeal was over.

It has been recorded in several places that Clark and Hambleton eventually were extracted by South Vietnamese troops (says one account) or American Marines (says another) who worked their way upstream to reach the pair. In fact, Clark and Hambleton were extracted by the Navy Seal team which disguised itself as a party of Vietnamese sampan rivergoers. Throughout the operation, air cover by A-1 Skyraiders was a vital factor. Many details of the Seal rescue effort remain unavailable to this day.

The rescue of Hambleton and OV-10 survivor Mark Clark (NAIL 38B) eventually succeeded at the cost of 16 lives—six in the HH-53C, eight men aboard the two US Army helicopters shot down during the action, and two men aboard Cessna O-2A Skymaster 68-10842, call sign COVEY 82, which was also downed. Also part of the cost was the capture of NAIL 38A, Bill Henderson. The magnitude of the action and the heavy fighting in which Boli and other Skyraider pilots found themselves was typical of combat taking place during that period.

It has already been noted on these pages that the Douglas AD/A-1 Skyraider fought to the end in Vietnam. The Skyraider's final fight in the defence of Saigon has been covered. Although they captured large numbers of South Vietnamese aircraft when they took over, the communists apparently never made any attempt to employ surviving Skyraiders. Today, no Skyraiders remain in service as active combat aircraft with any air force in the world, although non-flying examples are strewn all over Africa where the AD/A-1 once flew and fought.

Warbird A-1

Today, numerous Skyraiders are available for examination in museums, displayed as gate guards, and (increasingly) flying as restored warbirds on the airshow circuit. So far, the AD-4 seems to be the most advanced variant to appear as a flying warbird, although several aeroplanes of this mark have been painted as Vietnam-era A-1H (AD-6) aircraft.

In all other respects, the Skyraider is history. Like the willingness of free people to use force when necessary—a willingness never lacked by Skyraider pilots, whatever the risk—the Skyraider is a thing of the past. Perhaps this is apt. The brave men who flew and fought in the Skyraider in Korea, Vietnam and elsewhere can only be appalled by today's splintered population of narrow, special interests and by the reluctance of a new generation of Americans to employ force of arms when need is. When Charles Vasiliadis, Bernie Fisher, Jim Burden and Fred Boli were growing up, it would never have been imagined that a great and free nation would allow its citizens to be held hostage, would permit itself to be kicked around by others who lack both greatness and freedom—would be unwilling, when the need is there, to fight. As an American phenomenon, the Skyraider is rather like the much-mentioned American century. It came and went, and we allowed it to slip through our fingers.

Readers of this volume and of other works in this Air Combat series will know that success in battle is a combination of many things and that in aerial warfare success depends upon the right mixture of man, airplane and circumstance. When the Skyraider was designed overnight in a hotel room, it was the right airplane for the right time and its long years of service have proven this rightness again and again. During the period in our history when men were assigned to fly into the crucible at the controls of a Skyraider, there was never any doubt that we had the right men for the job: their courage and sacrifice was demonstrated again and again. We have 'right' airplanes and courageous men today, but something has gone wrong with the third factor in the equation, the circumstances which enable us to fight and win.

This account of the Skyraider and its times is this author's final work in this series and his final attempt to sketch on paper the history of a single aircraft type. Future efforts will probably be devoted less to aviation history and more to the issue of whether, and when, our tools and people will be employed in combat. The opportunity to examine five aircraft types in this series has been a special privilege and pleasure, not soon to be forgotten. To others who will produce histories of military aircraft in days ahead, this author urges the obvious: the story cannot be told without remembering that there is always a man in the cockpit and a war, out there, to be won.

As for the pilot used in this chapter to typify all those who flew Ed Heinemann's quaking, smoke-belching, oil-dripping aeroplane, Colonel Fred C Boli has a precise and detailed list of his 111 combat missions in the A-1 Skyraider, including several combat rescues. His last mission took place on 11 May 1972, in A-1E Skyraider 134577 rather than the single-seat A-1H/J he usually flew. As a senior Air Force officer today, Fred Boli can look with satisfaction at a long career, but no other experience compares with his days flying the Skyraider in combat. Says he, 'It was an extraordinary experience.'

*Pilot of this US Air Force A-1H Skyraider of the 602nd
SOS adds a touch of throttle to ease his mount onto the
taxiway prior to taking off from 'NKP', Thailand
(USAF)*

Postscript

This book is dedicated to the memory of Douglas Remington of Seattle, Washington, who did much to preserve the history of military aviation.

Mistakes are solely the fault of the author but *Douglas A-1 Skyraider* would have been impossible without the assistance of many who contributed to these pages.

I especially want to thank the British Aviation Group (BARG) for permission to quote from the out-of-print monograph, *A History of the Douglas Skyraider AEW.1*.

I would also like to thank Hal Andrews, Dennis Baldry, William F Brabant, Jim Burden, Mike Byers, James Doolittle 3rd, Michael J Dugan, Victor Flintham, Doug Francis, Harry Gann, Perrin Gower, Joseph G Handelman, DDS, Paul Jackson, Hubert G King, Robert L Lawson, Lars-Erik Lundin, David W Menard, Peter B Mersky, R J Mills Jr, Albert Mongeon, David Ostrowski, Glyn Owen, Chris Pocock, Norman Polmar, the gang at Roy's, Paul D Stevens, Martin Swann, Norman Taylor, 'Deep Throat', and Nick Williams.

Robert F Dorr
Oakton, Virginia, July 1988

Appendices

Appendix I. BT2D and AD Skyraiders manufactured

Model	Amount	From	To	Remarks
BT2D-1	25	09085	09109	Originally XBT2D-1; 1 (09096) converted to BT2D-1P; 2 (09098/09099) converted to BT2D-1N; 1 (09109) converted to BT2D-1Q; redesignated AD-1 2/1/46; 1 (09107) converted to XAD-1W; 1 (09108) converted to XAD-2
AD-1	242	09110	09351	
AD-1Q	35	09352	09386	
AD-2	156	122210	122365	
AD-2Q	22	122366	122387	1 (122373) converted to AD-2QU
AD-3	125	122729	122853	1 (122853) converted to AD-4
AD-3Q	23	122854	122876	Originally AD-3QU
AD-3W	31	122877	122907	2 (122906/122907) converted to AD-3E
AD-3N	15	122908	122922	2 (122910/122911) converted to AD-3s
AD-4	372	123771	124006	63 (123935; 123592/124005; 127845/127852) converted to AD-4L
	(30)	(124007)	(124036)*	
		127844	127879	28 (127866; 127868/127872; 128937/128943; 128971/128978) converted to AD-4B
		128917	129016	1 (124006) converted to AD-5
AD-4N	307	124128	124156	100 (125742/125764; 126876/126883; 126903/126925; 126947/126969; 126988/127010) converted to AD-4NA which redesignated A-1D 9/18/62
		124725	124760	
		125707	125764	
		126876	127018	
		127880	127926	37 (124153, 124725/124760) converted to AD-4NL
AD-4W	168	124976	124127	50 transferred to Royal Navy (Britain) of which 14 transferred to Sweden
		124761	124777	
		125765	125782	
		126836	126875	
		127921	127961	
AD-4Q	39	124037	124075	
AD-4B	165	132227	132391	
	(14)	(134005)	(134018)*	
AD-5	212	132748	Redesignated A-1E 9/18/62; some AD-5 target tow aircraft redesignated UA-1E	
		132392	132476	
		132637	132686	9/18/62
	(75)	(133930)	(134004)*	
	(158)	(134076)	(134233)	

AD-5N	239	132477		2 (132506, 135054) factory-converted
		132480	132636	and 54 field-converted to AD-5Q which
	(32)	(132637)	(132668)*	redesignated EA-1F 9/18/62
	(60)	(235055)	(135138)*	
AD-5W	218	132729		Redesignated EA-1E 9/18/62
	(84)	(132730)	(132792)*	
		133757	133776	
	135139	135222		
	(34)	(138535)	(138568)*	
		139556	139605	
AD-5s	1	132479		
AD-6	713	134466	134537	Redesignated A-1H 9/18/62
		135223	135406	
		137492	137632	
		139606	139821	
AD-7	72	142010	142081	Redesignated A-1J 9/18/62
Total	3,180			

* = cancelled

Appendix 2. AD-4W Skyraider AEW.1 delivered to the Royal Navy

Bureau Number	British Serial
124080	WV104
124085	WV103
124086	WV106
124101	WV177
124107	WT969
124110	WV107
124111	WV178
124112	WT112
124113	WV105
124114	WT964
124115	WV179
124116	WV180
124121	WT121
124122	WV102
124124	WT965
124761	WT761
124765	WT966
124768	WT968
124771	WT967
First Batch:	19
124097	WT097
124103	WT986
124104	WT985
124774	WT944
124777	WT947
125772	WV183
126846	WV184
126849	WT849
126866	WT984
126867	WV181
127922	WT987
Second batch:	11
124774	WT944
124775	WT945
124776	WT946
124777	WT947
Third Batch:	4
127946	WT948
127947	WT949
127948	WT950
127949	WT951
127950	WT952
127951	WT953
127952	WT954
127953	WT955
127954	WT956
127955	WT957
127956	WT958
127957	WT959
127958	WT960
127959	WT961
127960	WT962
127961	WT963
Fourth Batch:	16
Total:	50

British Serial	Bureau Number
WT097	124097
WT112	124112
WT121	124121
WT761	124761
WT849	126849
WT944	124774
WT945	124775
WT946	124776
WT947	124777
WT948	127946
WT949	127947
WT950	127948
WT951	127949
WT952	127950
WT953	127951
WT954	127952
WT955	127953
WT956	127954
WT957	127955
WT958	127956
WT959	127957
WT960	127958
WT961	127959
WT962	127960
WT963	127961
WT964	124112
WT965	124124
WT966	124765
WT967	124771
WT968	124768
WT969	124107
WT984	126866
WT985	124104
WT986	124103
WT986	124103
WT987	127922
WV102	124122
WV103	124085
WV104	124080
WV105	124113
WV106	124086
WV107	124110
WV177	124101
WV178	124111
WV179	124115
WV180	124116
WV181	126867
WV182	127942
WV183	125772
WV184	126846
WV185	127945
Total:	50

Index